Introduction to Epidemiology

Understanding Public Health

Series editors: Nick Black and Rosalind Raine, London School of Hygiene & Tropical Medicine

Throughout the world, recognition of the importance of public health to sustainable, safe and healthy societies is growing. The achievements of public health in nineteenth-century Europe were for much of the twentieth century overshadowed by advances in personal care, in particular in hospital care. Now, with the dawning of a new century, there is increasing understanding of the inevitable limits of individual health care and of the need to complement such services with effective public health strategies. Major improvements in people's health will come from controlling communicable diseases, eradicating environmental hazards, improving people's diets and enhancing the availability and quality of effective health care. To achieve this, every country needs a cadre of knowledgeable public health practitioners with social, political and organizational skills to lead and bring about changes at international, national and local levels.

This is one of a series of 20 books that provides a foundation for those wishing to join in and contribute to the twenty-first-century regeneration of public health, helping to put the concerns and perspectives of public health at the heart of policy-making and service provision. While each book stands alone, together they provide a comprehensive account of the three main aims of public health: protecting the public from environmental hazards, improving the health of the public and ensuring high quality health services are available to all. Some of the books focus on methods, others on key topics. They have been written by staff at the London School of Hygiene & Tropical Medicine with considerable experience of teaching public health to students from low, middle and high income countries. Much of the material has been developed and tested with postgraduate students both in face-to-face teaching and through distance learning.

The books are designed for self-directed learning. Each chapter has explicit learning objectives, key terms are highlighted and the text contains many activities to enable the reader to test their own understanding of the ideas and material covered. Written in a clear and accessible style, the series will be essential reading for students taking postgraduate courses in public health and will also be of interest to public health practitioners and policy-makers.

Titles in the series

Analytical models for decision making: Colin Sanderson and Reinhold Gruen
Controlling communicable disease: Norman Noah
Economic analysis for management and policy: Stephen Jan, Lilani Kumaranayake, Jenny Roberts, Kara Hanson and Kate Archibald
Economic evaluation: Julia Fox-Rushby and John Cairns (eds)
Environmental epidemiology: Paul Wilkinson (ed)
Environment, health and sustainable development: Megan Landon
Environmental health policy: Megan Landon and Tony Fletcher
Financial management in health services: Reinhold Gruen and Anne Howarth
Global change and health: Kelley Lee and Jeff Collin (eds)
Health care evaluation: Sarah Smith, Don Sinclair, Rosalind Raine and Barnaby Reeves
Health promotion practice: Maggie Davies, Wendy Macdowall and Chris Bonell (eds)
Health promotion theory: Maggie Davies and Wendy Macdowall (eds)
Introduction to epidemiology: Lucianne Bailey, Katerina Vardulaki, Julia Langham and Daniel Chandramohan
Introduction to health economics: David Wonderling, Reinhold Gruen and Nick Black
Issues in public health: Joceline Pomerleau and Martin McKee (eds)
Making health policy: Kent Buse, Nicholas Mays and Gill Walt
Managing health services: Nick Goodwin, Reinhold Gruen and Valerie Iles
Medical anthropology: Robert Pool and Wenzel Geissler
Principles of social research: Judith Green and John Browne (eds)
Understanding health services: Nick Black and Reinhold Gruen

Introduction to Epidemiology

Lucianne Bailey, Katerina Vardulaki,
Julia Langham and Daniel Chandramohan

Open University Press

Open University Press
McGraw-Hill Education
McGraw-Hill House
Shoppenhangers Road
Maidenhead
Berkshire
England
SL6 2QL

email: enquiries@openup.co.uk
world wide web: www.openup.co.uk

and Two Penn Plaza, New York, NY 10121-2289, USA

First published 2005
Reprinted 2006 (twice), 2007 (twice), 2008
Copyright © London School of Hygiene & Tropical Medicine 2005

A catalogue record of this book is available from the British Library

ISBN-10: 0 335 21833 4
ISBN-13: 978 0335 21833 2
Library of Congress Cataloging-in-Publication Data
CIP data applied for

Typeset by RefineCatch Limited, Bungay, Suffolk
Printed in the UK by Bell & Bain Ltd, Glasgow

Contents

Acknowledgements

Open University Press and the London School of Hygiene and Tropical Medicine have made every effort to obtain permission from copyright holders to reproduce material in this book and to acknowledge these sources correctly. Any omissions brought to our attention will be remedied in future editions.

We would like to express our grateful thanks to the following copyright holders for granting permission to reproduce material in this book.

p. 55–56 S Abdulla, J Armstrong Schellenberg, R Nathan, O Mukasa, T Marchant, T Smith, M Tanner and C Lengeler, *British Medical Journal*, 2001, 322:269–273, amended with permission from the BMJ Publishing Group.

p. 21 © Lucianne Bailey 2004. Reproduced with permission from Lucianne Bailey.

p. 9 Reproduced by permission of the Centers for Disease Control and Prevention.

p. 116–7, 120–1 G Rose, The Strategy of Preventive Medicine, 1992, Oxford University Press.

p. 8 Based on KJ Rothman, 'Causes', *American Journal of Epidemiology*, 1976, 104(6):587–592 by permission of Oxford University Press.

p. 62 A Schatzkin, S Piantadosi, M Miccozzi and D Bartee, 'Alcohol consumption and breast cancer: a cross-national correlation study,' *International Journal of Epidemiology*, 1989, 18(1): 28–31, by permission of Oxford University Press.

p. 11–17 *Snow on Cholera: being a reprint of two papers by John Snow, M.D., together with a Biographical Memoir by B.W. Richardson, M.D. and an Introduction by Wade Hampton Frost, M.D.*, London, Oxford University Press, 1936.

p. 59 SV Subramanian, S Nandy, M Kelly, D Gordon and G Davey Smith, 'Patterns and distribution of tobacco consumption in India: cross sectional multilevel evidence from the 1998–9 national family health survey,' *British Medical Journal*, 2004, 328:801–506, with permission from the BMJ Publishing Group.

p. 6 A Taranta and M Markowitz, *Rheumatic fever: a guide to its recognition, prevention and cure, 2nd ed.*, 1989, Kluwer Academic Publishers, by permission of Springer.

p. 27–8 Data from WHO IARC Cancer Mortality Statistics 2004 and CancerMondial http://www-dep.iarc.fr/

Overview of the book

Introduction

This book provides a summary of the main methods and concepts of epidemiology to enable you to understand, interpret and apply these basic methods. It also aims to introduce more advanced epidemiological and statistical concepts.

It is not the intention that epidemiology should be viewed as a solitary field, as it is integral to much of public health.

Why study epidemiology?

Epidemiology provides the tools (scientific methods) to study the causes of disease and the knowledge base for health care. Thus it provides public health professionals the means to study disease and look at the effectiveness of health care services and, more specifically, the impact of health care interventions.

It provides one key approach to understanding health and disease in individuals and populations, and the forces and factors which influence them. This is important both for health care professionals and for patients. The purpose of epidemiology is to use this information to promote health and reduce disease.

Clinical practice and health policy cannot be based on clinical experience alone. They need to be based on scientific evidence. Understanding epidemiology and the methods used to study health and disease is a prerequisite for the ability to appraise critically the evidence in scientific literature. The ability to distinguish good from poor science (and good and poor evidence) is an essential skill in promoting evidence-based health care.

Epidemiology is one of the key scientific disciplines underlying some of the most important and rapidly developing areas of inquiry into health and health care. Epidemiological methods are central to clinical research, disease prevention, health promotion, health protection and health services research. The results of epidemiological studies are also used by other scientists, including health economists, health policy analysts, and health services managers.

Structure of the book

This book follows the conceptual framework of the basic epidemiology unit at the London School of Hygiene & Tropical Medicine. It is based on materials presented in the lectures and seminars of the taught course, which have been adapted for distance learning.

The book is structured around the basic concepts and applications of epidemiology. It starts by looking at definitions of epidemiology, introduces the fundamental strategies for measuring disease frequency and patterns of disease, and associations with exposures or risk factors (Chapters 1–3).

Chapters 4–8 discuss different study designs and their strengths and weaknesses. Analysis and interpretation of epidemiological studies are addressed in Chapter 9.

The final three chapters (10–12) outline the application of epidemiology for prevention, monitoring and screening.

The 12 chapters are shown on the contents page. Each chapter includes:

- an overview
- a list of learning objectives
- a list of key terms
- a range of activities
- feedback on the activities
- a summary.

Acknowledgements

The authors thank colleagues who developed the original lectures and teaching materials at the London School of Hygiene & Tropical Medicine on which the contents are based, Professor Ross Anderson, St George's Hospital Medical School, for reviewing the entire book, and Deirdre Byrne (series manager) for help and support.

Basic concepts and applications of epidemiology

Overview

Epidemiology is a basic science of public health. Its principles and methods are used to: describe the health of populations; detect causes of health problems; quantify the association between ill health and determinants; test treatments and public health interventions; and monitor changes in states of health over time. The key feature of epidemiology is that it is a study of populations, not individuals. In this chapter you will learn the basic concepts and applications of this discipline.

Learning objectives

After working through this chapter, you will be better able to:

- **describe the key aspects of the epidemiological approach**
- **discuss the models of causation of disease**
- **describe the natural history of disease**
- **discuss the applications of epidemiology in public health practice.**

Studying epidemiology

Epidemiology is the study of the distribution and determinants of health states or events in specified populations, and the application of this study to control health problems. It is concerned with the collective health of people in a community or an area and it provides data for directing public health action. Given the definition above, it follows that knowledge of the distribution and determinants of health states and events informs appropriate public health action.

What is the distribution of health states or events?

The *distribution* of health states or events is a description of the frequency and pattern of health events in a population. The *frequency* (e.g. the number of occurrences of a health event in a population within a given time period) is measured by rates and risks of health events in a population, and the *pattern* refers to the occurrence of health-related events by time, place and personal characteristics. (Rates and risks will be discussed more in Chapters 2 and 3).

What are determinants of health states or events?

Epidemiology seeks to identify the determinants of health and determinants of disease. The determinants of health states or events are definable factors that influence the occurrence of health-related events. Determinants are also known as risk factors or protective factors, depending on which health-related events they are associated with. Health-related events refer to health outcomes (e.g. death, illness and disability) as well as positive health states (e.g. survival and reduced risk of stroke), and the means to improve health.

The epidemiological approach

Like detectives, epidemiologists investigate health-related events in a rigorous way. An epidemiologist's approach to studying these events involves answering the questions:

- what?
- who?
- where?
- when?
- why?

These questions can be referred to as:

- case definition
- person
- place
- time
- causes

What?

A *case definition* is a set of standard criteria for deciding whether or not a person has a particular disease or health-related event. A case definition consists of clinical criteria, sometimes with limitations on time, place and person. The clinical criteria usually include confirmatory laboratory tests, if available, or a combination of symptoms (complaints) and signs (physical findings), and other supportive evidence. For example, in the USA, the case definition for paralytic poliomyelitis used by the Centers for Disease Control and Prevention (CDC 1992: 461) is: 'Acute onset of a flaccid paralysis of one or more limbs with decreased or absent tendon reflexes in the affected limbs, without other apparent cause, and without sensory or cognitive loss'. Application of standard criteria ensures that every case is diagnosed in the same way regardless of when and where it occurred. This allows comparison of rates of occurrence of the disease between populations and over time.

A case definition may have several sets of criteria, depending on how certain the diagnosis is. For example, during an outbreak of measles, you may classify a person with fever and rash as a suspected case of measles; one with fever, rash and a history of contact with a confirmed case of measles as a probable case of measles; and one with fever, rash and a positive serologic test for measles IgM antibody as a confirmed case of measles.

A case definition may also include *exclusion criteria* to exclude people even if they meet the criteria for a case. For example, cases may be excluded on the basis of their age.

Who?

Counting the number of *persons* involved in a health event is one of the basic first steps in an epidemiological investigation. However, a simple count of cases is inadequate for comparing the occurrence of disease in different populations or during different times, so case counts are converted into risks or rates, which relate the number of cases to the size of the population (you will learn more about risks and rates in Chapter 2).

People differ in certain inherent characteristics (e.g. age, ethnic group, sex), acquired characteristics (e.g. immunity, nutrition), socioeconomic conditions (e.g. education, occupation, housing), or health-related beliefs and behaviours (e.g. tobacco or alcohol consumption, health care seeking). Since personal attributes are often associated with health events, differences in the distribution of these factors should also be considered while comparing occurrence of health events between populations.

Where?

Health events are described by *place* to gain insight into the geographical difference or extent of the event. The place can be, for example, place of residence, birth or employment, a district, a state, or a country, depending on what is appropriate to the occurrence of the health event. Analysis of data by place can also give clues as to the source of agents that cause disease and their mode of transmission. A spot map is a map on which each case is related to a specific type of place, such as a place of work; such maps can be useful in identifying the source of the causal agent while investigating an outbreak.

When?

Rates of occurrence of disease often change over *time*. Plotting the annual rate of a disease over a period of years can show the long term or secular trends in the occurrence of the disease. These trends can be used to help predict the future incidence of a disease and also to evaluate programmes or policy decisions, or to suggest what caused an increase or decrease in the occurrence of a disease. Figure 1.1 is an example of such a graph.

✎ Activity 1.1

Figure 1.1 shows a declining trend in the incidence of rheumatic fever in Denmark since 1900. The incidence drops particularly sharply after 1900, having been quite steady for the previous 40 years. What might this suggest?

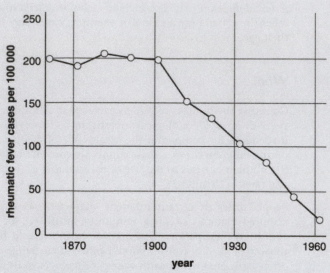

Figure 1.1 Incidence of rheumatic fever in Denmark, 1862–1962

Source: from Beaglehole *et al.* (1993)

 Feedback

The nature of the curve suggests that some event or action might well have triggered the decline in the incidence of rheumatic fever around 1900.

Rheumatic fever is caused by haemolytic streptococcal infection, which is associated with poverty and overcrowding. It is, therefore, plausible to attribute the decline in rheumatic fever to the improvement in socioeconomic conditions in Denmark that occurred at the beginning of the twentieth century.

Graphs of the occurrence of a disease by week or month, over the course of a year or more, show its seasonal pattern. Some diseases are known to have typical seasonal patterns; for example, the incidence of influenza increases in winter.

Why?

In addition to describing the levels and patterns in the occurrence of health events by person, place and time, epidemiology is concerned with the search for causes and effects. Epidemiologists quantify the association between potential determinants of health states and health events, and test hypotheses about causality and associations between the determinants and health events. There are several epidemiological study designs, but their shared basic principle is to make an unbiased comparison between a group with and a group without the determinant or health event under investigation (study designs are dealt with in detail in Chapters 4–8).

Models of causation of disease

In order to understand the principles and applications of epidemiology, you need to know the potential processes and pathways by which various factors can lead to ill health. There are several models of causation that have been proposed to help the understanding of disease processes. In epidemiology, the models widely applied are:

- the epidemiological triad
- the sufficient cause and component causes model

The epidemiological triad

The epidemiological triad or triangle is the traditional model of causation of infectious diseases (Figure 1.2). It is based on three components: an external *agent*, a susceptible *host*, and an *environment* that facilitates interaction between the host and the agent. The agent might be a microorganism such as a virus, bacterium or parasite; or a chemical substance. Host factors are the intrinsic factors that influence an individual's exposure, susceptibility, or response to a causative agent: for example, age, sex, ethnic group, and behaviour are some of the factors that determine an individual's risk of exposure to an agent; age, genetic composition, nutritional and immunological status are some of the factors that influence individual susceptibility and response to an agent. The environmental factors are extrinsic factors that affect the agent and the opportunity for exposure. They include physical factors (e.g. climate, geological characteristics), biological factors (e.g. vectors – insects that transmit an agent) and structural factors (e.g. crowding, and availability of health and sanitation services).

Agent, host and environmental factors are interrelated in many ways. The balance and interactions between them that lead to the occurrence of disease in humans vary for different diseases.

This model can work for some non-infectious diseases, but there can be difficulties because certain factors are not easily classified as agents or environmental factors.

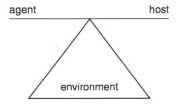

Figure 1.2 The epidemiological triad

Sufficient cause and component causes model

A *sufficient cause* is a set of factors or conditions that inevitably produces disease. The factors or conditions that form a sufficient cause are called *component causes*. Component causes include host factors, agents and environmental factors. If a disease does not develop without the presence of a particular component cause, then that component cause is classified as a necessary cause. However, a single component cause, even if it is a necessary cause, is rarely a sufficient cause by itself.

For example, exposure to the infectious agent *Mycobacterium tuberculosis* is a necessary cause for tuberculosis, but it is not sufficient as it does not always result in disease (some people may not develop the disease or may become carriers). Whether a person develops a disease or not depends on other component factors which determine their susceptibility, such as their immune status, concurrent conditions (e.g. HIV infection, diabetes, silicosis), genetic factors, age and socio-economic status. Similarly, smoking is a component cause for lung cancer (smoking increases the risk of lung cancer). However, smoking is not a sufficient cause because not all people who smoke develop lung cancer; nor is it a necessary cause because lung cancer can develop in non-smokers.

 Activity 1.2

Three sufficient causes (1, 2 and 3) and their component causes (denoted by letters) of a hypothetical disease are shown in Figure 1.3. If there are no other sufficient causes of this disease, which component cause is a necessary cause?

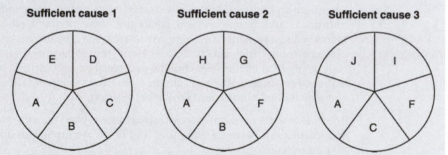

Figure 1.3 Conceptual scheme of three sufficient causes of a hypothetical disease
Source: based on Rothman (2002)

 Feedback

Component cause A is the necessary cause since this factor is part of all three sufficient causes; it must be present in combination with other factors for this disease to occur.

If Figure 1.3 were a representation of the only sufficient causes of tuberculosis, then *Mycobacterium tuberculosis* would be represented by component cause A, the necessary cause. Other factors such as immunity, concurrent illness, genetic and socioeconomic factors would be represented by components B, C, D, E, F, G, H, I and J.

On the other hand, if Figure 1.3 were a representation of some of the sufficient causes of lung cancer, then smoking could be represented by B which is present in sufficient causes 1 and 2, but not in 3. Sufficient cause 3 may be the cause of lung cancer in individuals who do not smoke.

This conceptual scheme is able to show that a disease can occur from different sufficient causes, and that component causes may be unknown (as is often the case in non-communicable diseases). The scheme also demonstrates that it is not necessary to identify every component of a sufficient cause in order to prevent a disease; a disease can be prevented by eliminating *any single component cause* since this prevents completion of a sufficient cause. For example, eliminating smoking (component B) would prevent lung cancer from sufficient causes 1 and 2, although some lung cancer would still occur from sufficient cause 3.

Natural history of disease

The *natural history of disease* refers to the progress of the disease process in an individual over time and in the absence of intervention (Figure 1.4). Knowledge of the natural history of a disease helps us to understand the effects and mechanism of actions, potential interventions, and the different levels of the prevention of disease.

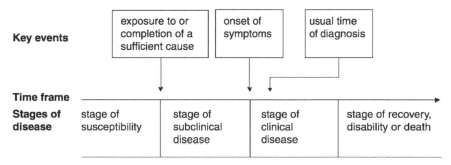

Figure 1.4 Natural history of disease
Source: based on CDC (1992)

The *disease process* begins with exposure to, or completion of, a sufficient cause of the disease. Without an appropriate intervention, the process ends with recovery, disability or death. For example, exposure to the measles virus in a susceptible individual initiates the stage of subclinical disease. The onset of fever on about the 10th day (range 7–18 days) after exposure marks the beginning of clinical disease. The disease, however, is usually diagnosed around the 14th day when the typical rashes appear and then the disease proceeds to recovery, to complications such as pneumonia, or to death, depending on host and other factors.

Many diseases have a typical natural history, but the time frame and manifestations of disease may vary between individuals due to the presence of host factors (e.g. immunity and age) and other determinants of the disease. Many factors may affect the progress of a disease in an individual and the likely outcome. The estimation of an individual's outcome, taking into account the natural history of disease and other risk factors, is known as their *prognosis*.

The course of a disease may also be modified at any point in the progression by preventive and therapeutic measures. The subclinical stage following exposure is usually called the *incubation period* (for infectious diseases) or the *latency period* (for chronic diseases).

Applications of epidemiology in public health

Epidemiological principles, methods, tools and information are applied in every aspect of public health from policy setting at a macro level to decision making at individual level. The brief discussions that follow, although not exhaustive, will give you an idea of the spectrum of application of epidemiology in public health.

Community health assessment and priority setting

In order to set priorities and appropriate policies, and be able to plan programmes, public heath professionals need answers to questions like the following:

* What are the actual and potential health problems in the community?
* Where and among whom are they occurring or would they occur?
* Which problems are increasing or decreasing, or have the potential to increase or decrease over time?
* How do the levels and patterns of health problems relate to the existing health services?

Epidemiological methods and tools provide answers to these and other related questions and help decision making for health policies and programmes.

Evaluating health interventions and programmes

Epidemiological studies of the *efficacy* (how well a health intervention works under ideal conditions) and *effectiveness* (how well a health intervention works under usual conditions) of health interventions provide important information for identifying appropriate interventions. Ongoing surveillance of diseases is essential to ensure the continued safety and effectiveness of health interventions. Epidemiological principles and methods are also used in evaluating health policies and programmes.

Preventing disease and promoting health

Epidemiological studies contribute to the understanding of the causes, modes of transmission, natural histories and control measures of diseases. This understanding is essential for developing appropriate health promotion strategies to prevent disease perhaps in those most at risk, or as a population-wide effort by tackling known causes. Studies can provide information on the effectiveness of health promotion interventions and identify for whom they are most effective to help direct resources.

Improving diagnosis, treatment and prognosis of clinical disease

Epidemiological research contributes to identification of appropriate tests and criteria for diagnosis and screening. It is important to know the diagnostic accuracy of tests, that is, how well a test can discriminate between those with and without the disease (you will learn more about diagnostic accuracy and screening in Chapter 11). Epidemiological research can help determine the most effective treatment in a given situation and the likely outcome of patients, which is essential for planning care.

Activity 1.3

You have been given a lot of material to take in; some of it is intuitive, some less so. In order to help you put these ideas in context, you will now look at a famous example from the nineteenth century.

John Snow (1813–58) was a distinguished physician. As an epidemiologist, he is best known for his studies of cholera, in particular of two outbreaks that occurred in London in 1848–9 and 1854. This exercise is based on his work and illustrates the epidemiological approach from descriptive epidemiology to hypothesis generation and testing, and the application of epidemiological data.

Activities 1.3–1.7 are interrelated and use John Snow's cholera studies as an example. Feedback follows each activity so that you are prepared for the next one, but don't read the feedback until you have tried to answer the question for yourself. The answers given in the feedback are not the only 'correct' answers. There are many ways to approach these questions, and your answers can be different from those given in the feedback.

Cholera periodically swept across Europe during the nineteenth century. After a severe epidemic in 1832, the disease next appeared in London in 1848. The first definite case of the outbreak occurred in September 1848 and was that of John Harnold, a seaman of the ship *Elbe*, newly arrived from Hamburg where cholera was prevalent. Mr Harnold died a few hours after the onset of symptoms on 22 September in a lodge near the River Thames. The next case occurred in the same room; Mr Blenkinsopp, who lodged in the room, had cholera on 30 September. During the epidemic approximately 15,000 deaths were recorded. The mortality from cholera in this epidemic was particularly high in residential areas downstream, but decreased progressively upstream. Since water must flow downhill, upstream areas are, of course, at lower risk than those further downstream.

Snow had previously documented several circumstances in which people who had come into contact with cases of cholera developed the disease within a few days. While investigating several case series of cholera, he had made the following observations:

- Cholera was more readily transmitted in poor households and to those who had handled a case of cholera.
- The mining population had suffered more than people in any other occupation.
- Almost no physician who attended to cholera cases or did post-mortems had developed cholera.

- Most cases of cholera developed within 24–48 hours after contact with a case of cholera.
- The disease was characterized by profuse painless diarrhoea and often proceeded with so little feeling of general illness that the patient did not consider himself in danger, or seek advice, until the malady was far advanced.

Based on these observations, Snow postulated the following hypotheses on the mode of transmission of cholera:

- Cholera can be transmitted from the sick to the healthy.
- Cholera is caused by some material (Snow called it 'morbid matter') which has the property of increasing and multiplying in the body of the person it attacks.
- The 'morbid matter' producing cholera must be introduced into the alimentary canal by swallowing.
- The 'morbid matter' may be transmitted through water from the sick to the healthy.

Microorganisms had not yet been discovered and one of the popular beliefs about the causation of disease was the theory of 'miasma' – that breathing 'bad air' caused disease.

1   How do you think Snow interpreted his observations to test his hypotheses and to refute the miasma theory?

2   What are the plausible explanations for the observed association between the elevation of the residential area and the level of mortality from cholera?

 Feedback

1   Snow argued that the risk of transmission of cholera was high in miners and other people of lower socioeconomic status because these groups had poor hygiene practices and were, therefore, more likely to have contact with faecal matter from cholera patients (especially through wet linen) than those of higher socioeconomic status. On the other hand, not many physicians developed the disease because they washed their hands after seeing each cholera patient. If the transmission were through air or a vector, the disease would have been transmitted from cholera patients to more physicians. Thus, the disease must be caused by some form of 'morbid matter' that is transmitted by direct contact.

Citing the observation that there were very few or no signs of general illness at the beginning of the disease, Snow proposed that the 'morbid matter' must be multiplying in the alimentary canal rather than in the blood. If the 'morbid matter' were transmitted by direct contact because of poor hygiene practices, and if the 'morbid matter' multiplied in the gut, then swallowing the 'morbid matter' would produce the disease.

2   The observed association between the elevation of area of residence and mortality from cholera could support the theory of bad air causing cholera. However, Snow argued that the water downstream was more likely to be polluted with sewage than the water upstream. Thus, the increased risk of transmission of cholera in the areas downstream supported his theory that the 'morbid matter' was most probably transmitted through water.

Activity 1.4

During the nineteenth century, drinking water in London was supplied by private companies, which obtained water directly from the Thames. Each company had its own network of pipes and in some areas these networks overlapped to such an extent that the houses along a single street might be supplied by more than one company. The Southwark and Vauxhall (S & V) Company and the Lambeth Company were the two major companies that supplied water to cholera epidemic areas during these periods.

London was free of cholera from 1849 until 1853, and during this period the Lambeth Company moved its source of water upstream to an area outside London, while the S & V Company continued to draw water from a downstream source within London. When cholera reappeared in London in July 1853, Snow visited households where a cholera death had been recorded and collected information on the routine sources of water. The water sources for the households of the first 334 deaths are shown in Table 1.1.

Table 1.1 Water sources of households of people who died of cholera in London in 1853

Source of water	Number of deaths
S & V Company	286
Lambeth Company	14
Direct from river	26
Pump wells	4
Unknown	4
Total	334

Source: based on Snow (1936)

1 Do the data presented in this table support Snow's hypothesis that cholera is transmitted through water? Give reasons for your answer.

2 What further questions would you ask before reaching firm conclusions from these data?

 Feedback

1 Snow managed to collect information on the source of water for 330 of the 334 deaths (99%). This is a very high level of success in follow-up. Although people might have misreported the source of water, this would probably have been at random (the chance of misreporting would apply equally to all sources of water).

2 The data seem to suggest that cholera mortality was higher in households that were supplied by the S & V Company than in those supplied by the Lambeth Company. You might continue to argue that the increased mortality in the households supplied by the S & V Company was due to the company's water source being downstream and that therefore the data support Snow's hypothesis that cholera 'morbid matter' is

transmitted by water. However, although tempting, it is not appropriate to interpret the figures in this way, without asking the following fundamental questions:

a) How many households were supplied by the S & V Company and how many by the Lambeth Company?

b) What was the size of the populations supplied by each of these companies?

c) Were the two populations comparable in their socioeconomic status?

For instance, the S & V Company might have supplied water to more people than the Lambeth Company and this might explain the higher mortality in the population supplied by the S & V Company. It is also possible that since the S & V Company was drawing water from downstream, the households supplied by the company would have been in downstream areas and would be likely to be poorer than the households upstream. Thus, although these data appear to support Snow's hypothesis, more information is needed to be convincing.

 Activity 1.5

Snow collected data on the number of houses supplied by the S & V Company and the Lambeth Company. When the cholera epidemic recurred in London in 1854, he again collected data on sources of water in the houses of those who died of cholera. The number of cholera deaths per 10,000 houses during the first seven weeks of the epidemic (8 July to 26 August) in houses using different water sources is shown in Table 1.2.

Do you think these data are adequate to conclude that cholera mortality is higher in houses supplied by the S & V Company than in houses supplied by the Lambeth Company? Discuss your answer.

Table 1.2 Sources of water and cholera mortality in London, 9 July–26 August 1854

Source of water	Total number of households	Number of cholera deaths	Deaths per 10 000 houses
S & V Company	40 046	1 263	315
Lambeth Company	26 107	98	38
Other	256 423	1 422	55

Source: Snow (1936)

 Feedback

The risk of cholera death in houses supplied by the S & V Company was 315/10,000; in houses supplied by Lambeth Company it was 38/10,000; and in houses supplied by other sources it was 55/10,000. These data suggest that the risk of cholera death was 8–9 times as high (315/38) in houses supplied by the S & V Company as in houses supplied by the Lambeth Company. However, to reach this conclusion, it has to be assumed that the number of people per household, their socioeconomic status, and other potential factors associated with the risk of transmission of cholera are comparable between these two populations. This might not be the case; for instance, the S & V Company might have supplied water to multiple-occupancy buildings while Lambeth supplied individual houses. If this were the case, then the risk of cholera death per house between the two populations would not be comparable since the average number of people per house would differ between them.

Activity 1.6

Snow investigated a severe outbreak of cholera in the Soho area of London near his house. He collected the house addresses of all 616 recorded cholera deaths between 19 August and 30 September 1854. From these data he produced a spot map showing the distribution of cholera deaths and the positions of the water pumps (Figure 1.5).

Figure 1.5 Distribution of cholera cases around Golden Square, London, August–September 1854

Source: Snow (1936)

1   Using Figure 1.5, describe the distribution of cholera deaths in relation to the position of water pumps.

2   What explanations can you think of for the differences in the distribution of deaths around water pumps A, B and C?

3   Can you conclude that water from pump A was the source of the cholera epidemic?

4   What further information do you need?

↻ Feedback

1 Figure 1.5 shows that there was spatial clustering of deaths around pump A and very few deaths near pumps B and C.

2 If water from the pumps was the source of cholera, why were there fewer deaths around pumps B and C than around pump A? It is possible that people did not drink the water from pumps B and C for reasons such as bad taste or smell; the pumps might not have been conveniently situated for use; the water from these pumps might not have carried the 'morbid matter' of cholera.

3 The explanations in answer 2 are not sufficient information on which to conclude that pump A was the source of cholera; there are two blocks of buildings very close to pump A where there was not a single death from cholera.

4 Although water from pump A *might* be the source, more information is needed to explain the absence of death in the two blocks nearby before reaching this conclusion. It would only be possible to implicate the water from pump A as the source of the epidemic if it could be shown that there was no death in these blocks for reasons such as:

   a) no one lived there
   b) the inhabitants had alternative sources of water
   c) the inhabitants had some kind of protection against cholera.

✎ Activity 1.7

Snow discovered that a brewery was located in the two blockswith no deaths from cholera, and a deep well on the premises. The brewery workers and the people who lived close by collected water from the brewery well. In addition, the brewery workers had a daily quota of malt liquor. Snow was now convinced that pump A was the source of the cholera and he persuaded the local authorities to remove the pump. This was achieved on 8 September. The dates of onset of symptoms of the 616 fatal cases of cholera recorded between 19 August and 30 September are shown in Figure 1.6.

1   What does the graph in Figure 1.6 show?

2   Why do you think the epidemic stopped?

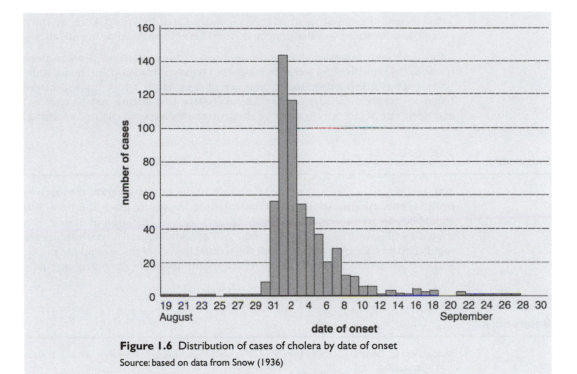

Figure 1.6 Distribution of cases of cholera by date of onset

Source: based on data from Snow (1936)

⟳ **Feedback**

1 There appears to have been a low background incidence of cases (zero or one case per day) before 30 August. There was an explosive rise in the number of cases over 3 days, which decreased to previous levels after 12 days. The most likely explanation for the sudden rise in the incidence of fatal cases of cholera would be exposure of the population to a causal agent from a common source.

2 There are several possible explanations for the cessation of the epidemic:

  a) People who lived in the area of epidemic might have moved out due to fear of contracting cholera.
  b) If all susceptible people had been exposed within a short time, there would be very few susceptible individuals remaining.
  c) The level of causal agent in the water could have been reduced.

It is unlikely that removal of pump A stopped the epidemic because the incidence of fatal cholera cases had already dropped almost to the background level by the time the pump was removed. However, another outbreak of cholera could have occurred if the number of susceptible individuals reached a critical point while the water from pump A contained the causal agent and was still available for use.

Vibrio cholera, the causal agent of cholera, was isolated by Robert Koch in 1883, several decades after Snow had concluded from his epidemiological investigations:

I feel confident, however, that by attending the above mentioned precautions (personal hygiene, boiling soiled bedclothes of patients, isolation and quarantine, improved waste disposal, drainage, provision of clear water), which I consider to be based on correct knowledge of the cause of cholera, this disease may be rendered extremely rare, if indeed it may not be altogether banished from civilized countries.

Summary

You should now be able to describe key aspects of the epidemiological approach to health events in terms of the event's distribution in person, place and time. You should be able to understand epidemiological models of causation of disease. You should be able to understand that results of epidemiological investigations are required to provide information about the natural history of disease and prognosis, and to help identify appropriate interventions and measures of control in public health.

References

Beaglehole R, Bonita R, Kjellstrom T (1993) *Basic Epidemiology*. Geneva: World Health Organization.
CDC (1992) *Principles of Epidemiology* (2nd edn). Atlanta, GA: Centers for Disease Control and Prevention.
Rothman K (2002) *Epidemiology: An Introduction*. Oxford: Oxford University Press.
Snow J (1936) *Snow on Cholera* (2nd edn). London: Oxford University Press.

2 Epidemiological measures of health and disease: frequency

Overview

The frequency of occurrence of disease, injury and death often varies over time and between populations. Epidemiological principles and methods are used to describe the frequency and the determinants of these events. In this chapter you will learn about the epidemiological measures that are used to quantify the frequency of morbidity and mortality in a population.

Learning objectives

After working through this chapter, you will be better able to:

- **define and calculate a range of measures of frequency of disease, including prevalence, risk, odds and rates**
- **define and calculate crude and specific mortality (morbidity) rates**
- **explain the limitations of comparing crude rates between populations and the methods to overcome these limitations.**

Key terms

Incidence The frequency of new cases in a defined population during a specified period of time.

Incidence risk (cumulative incidence) Calculated by dividing the number of new cases of a disease in a specified time period by the total population at risk during that period.

Prevalence The frequency of existing cases (e.g. of a disease) in a defined population at a particular point in time (point prevalence), or over a given period of time (period prevalence), as a proportion of the total population.

Definition of a case

In the previous chapter you learned about the basic concepts of epidemiology, and the components of the epidemiological approach. In this chapter, you will look more closely at these components, which were introduced by the questions 'what?', 'who?', 'where?', 'when?' and 'why?', and discover how they are used to answer questions that arise in epidemiological research.

To be able to quantify the occurrence of disease in populations, you will need to have a clear idea of what is meant by a *case*, that is, the person in a population who has a particular disease, or to whom the event of interest occurs (e.g. death). The case definition will in turn rely on the standard criteria used to identify that disease or event, and it may also be important to realize that any one person may experience more than one episode of a disease or event.

However, knowledge of the number of cases in a population is of little use on its own. We also need to know the size of the population from which the cases originate. For example, if you found that there were 75 cases of tuberculosis in village A and only 25 cases in village B, you might be tempted to conclude that tuberculosis was more common in village A than in village B. However, without knowing how many people live in each village, this comparison is impossible to make.

Measures of disease frequency

In this section, you will learn about the different ways to measure disease *frequency*. There are two main types of disease frequency – prevalence and incidence. Both measures relate to the number of cases in a population, and also include some concept of the time over which measurement is carried out.

Prevalence

Prevalence, or more correctly *point prevalence*, is the frequency of existing disease in a defined population at a particular point in time. It is measured by dividing the number of cases with the disease by the total number of people in the population at the same point in time:

$$\text{Point prevalence} = \frac{\text{Number of cases with disease at a point in time}}{\text{Total number of people in defined population at same point in time}}.$$

Although you should always specify the point in time to which point prevalence refers, prevalence is a proportion so it is dimensionless (i.e., it has no units). It is therefore inappropriate to use the term 'prevalence rate', even though this is common.

You may also see use of the term *period prevalence*. This refers to the number of people who were identified as cases at any time during a specified period of time (usually a short period), divided by the total number of people in that population. Period prevalence may also include people who became cases during that time period.

Incidence

Whereas prevalence is the frequency of *existing* cases of disease in a population, incidence is the frequency of *new* cases of disease in a defined population during a specified time period. Figure 2.1 shows how incidence and prevalence relate to one another. There are three different ways of measuring incidence.

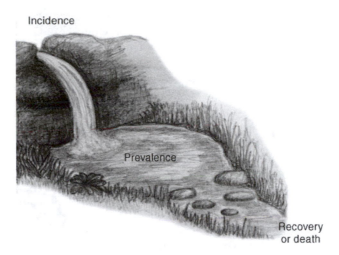

Incidence

Prevalence

Recovery
or death

Figure 2.1 Illustration of the relation between incidence and prevalence
© Lucianne Bailey 2004

Risk or cumulative incidence

The first measure of incidence is called *cumulative incidence*, or risk, since it refers to the occurrence of risk events (disease, injury or death) in a group of people studied over time. It is calculated in much the same way as prevalence, but rather than existing cases, only new cases are counted over the specified time interval. In this example, the risk event is disease:

$$\text{Cumulative incidence} = \frac{\text{Number of new cases with disease in a specified time period}}{\text{Number of disease-free people at the start of the time period}}.$$

It is important to note that the denominator is the total number of people who were free of disease at the start of the time period. This is defined as the 'population at risk'. Also note that, like prevalence, this measure is a proportion and is dimensionless. However, because cumulative incidence will increase over time, the time period over which it is measured must be clearly stated. For example, if a group of 100 people were studied for a year, and 25 had caught a cold at some point during the year, you would say that the risk of catching a cold was 0.25 or 25% in that year in that group.

Odds

Another way of measuring incidence is to calculate the *odds of disease*, injury or death. Rather than using the number of disease-free people at the beginning of the time period, odds are calculated by using the number of disease-free people at the end of the specified time:

$$\text{Odds of disease} = \frac{\text{Number of new cases with disease in a specified time period}}{\text{Number of people who were still disease-free by the end of the time period}}.$$

Like prevalence and cumulative incidence, this measure is dimensionless. However, rather than being a proportion, the odds are a ratio of two proportions:

$$\text{Odds of disease} = \frac{\text{Probability of getting the disease by the end of time period}}{\text{Probability of not getting the disease by the end of the time period}}.$$

Note that these formulae are equivalent, since the denominators used to calculate probabilities of getting or not getting disease will be identical and will therefore cancel each other out. In the example shown above, in which 25 people in a population of 100 caught a cold during a particular year, the odds of disease would be calculated by dividing 25 by 75 (or 25% divided by 75%), which gives an annual odds of 0.33 of catching a cold.

Incidence rate

Both risk and odds assume that the population at risk is followed over a specified time period, and that all those who are included at the beginning of the time period are counted at the end of the period. This is called a *closed* population or a *cohort*. However, you might want to look at incidence in a *dynamic* or *open* population over a longer period of time, during which people enter and exit the population at risk at different points. In this situation, people in the group may have been at risk for different lengths of time. Therefore, instead of counting the total number of people at the start of the study, the time that each individual spends in the study before becoming a case needs to be calculated. This is known as the person-time at risk and is illustrated in Figure 2.2.

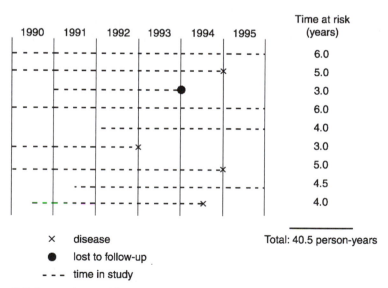

Figure 2.2 Person-time at risk

The incidence rate is obtained by dividing the number of people who have become cases by the person-time at risk:

$$\text{Incidence rate} = \frac{\text{Number of new cases with disease in a specified time period}}{\text{Total person-time at risk during that time period}}.$$

This measure of disease frequency is also known as *incidence density* or *force of morbidity* (or *force of mortality* if the event is death). Because person-time is used in the calculation of incidence rate, the incidence rate is stated as the number of new cases per person-time at risk, which might be person-days, person-months, person-years, or commonly per 100 person-years.

In the example shown in Figure 2.2, the incidence rate is obtained by dividing the total number of cases of disease by the total person-years of follow-up. Four people became cases during the study, so the incidence rate is 4/40.5 = 0.099 cases per person-year or 9.9 cases per 100 person-years of observation.

In much larger studies, where it might be difficult to measure the exact person-time for every individual in the study, the mid-period population can be used as an estimate for the total person-time at risk. In this situation, the average population at the mid-point of the calendar period of interest is multiplied by the number of years over which the study took place. Use of the mid-period population allows for people to enter and leave the study, as long as the population size does not change substantially over the study period and the incidence is low.

Now it is time for you to have a go. The following activity consists of several questions. If you find any question unclear or difficult, refer back to the text above while trying to answer. Try to complete all the questions before you look at the feedback.

Activity 2.1

One thousand men who were working in factory A were screened for HIV on 1 January 2002 and 50 of them were found to be positive for HIV antibodies. The screening was repeated in the same 1000 men on 1 January 2003 and this time 62 men were positive, including the 50 men who were positive on the first screening (no one had died or was lost to follow-up).

1   What is the prevalence of HIV in men working in factory A on 1 January 2002, and on 1 January 2003?

2   What is the annual risk of developing HIV infection in men working in factory A in 2002?

One thousand men from factory B were screened for HIV on 1 January 2002 and 50 men were found to be HIV-positive. All the men were tested for HIV once a month until 31 December 2002. Twelve men became HIV-positive during these 12 months. Figure 2.3 shows when these 12 men became HIV-positive. Tests were always carried out at the end of the month. The remaining 938 men were still HIV-negative by 31 December 2002. No one died or was lost to follow-up during this period.

3   What were the odds of becoming infected with HIV in the first 6 months of 2002 in the 12 men who became HIV-positive that year?

4   What is the total number of person-months at risk of HIV infection observed in this study?

5   What is the incidence rate of HIV infection in men working in factory B?

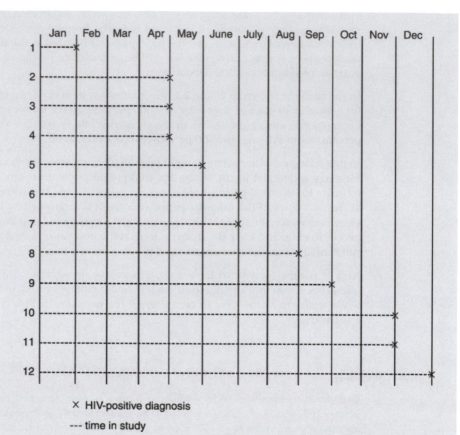

Figure 2.3 Person-months at risk contributed by the 12 men who became HIV-positive in 2002

⟳ **Feedback**

1 Number of prevalent cases at 1 January 2002 = 50.

Number of persons in the population in January 2002 = 1000.

Therefore, the prevalence at 1 January 2002 $= \dfrac{50}{1000} \times 100 = 5\%$.

Number of prevalent cases at 1 January 2003 = 62.

Number of persons in the population at 1 January 2003 = 1000.

Therefore, the prevalence at 1 January 2003 $= \dfrac{62}{1000} \times 100 = 6.2\%$.

2 Number of incident cases in 2002 = 12.

Number of persons at risk of HIV infection in January 2002 = 1000 − 50 = 950.

The annual risk of developing HIV infection $= \dfrac{12}{950} \times 100 = 1.26\%$.

The 50 men who were HIV-positive on 1 January 2002 are not included in the denominator. The reason for this exclusion is that HIV-positive individuals do not become HIV-negative, and therefore those who were HIV-positive on 1 January 2002 were not at risk of developing HIV infection during 2002.

3 Number of men who became HIV-positive in the first 6 months of 2002 = 7.
Number of men who did not become HIV-positive during first 6 months = 5.
Therefore, among those who became HIV-positive in 2002, the odds of becoming HIV-positive in the first 6 months = 7/5 = 1.4.

4 Person-months at risk contributed by HIV-negative men = $938 \times 12 = 11,256$.
Person-months at risk contributed by men infected at the beginning of study = 0.
Person-months at risk contributed by the 12 men infected during the study period =
$1 + (3 \times 4) + 5 + (2 \times 6) + 8 + 9 + (2 \times 11) + 12 = 81$.
Total person-months at risk observed = $11,256 + 81 = 11,337$.

5 To calculate the incidence rate you have to select an appropriate unit of person-time at risk for the denominator. In this example, person-months would be appropriate since the person-months at risk contributed by the men who were infected during the study period can be easily computed from the table.

Total number of incident cases = 12.

Incidence rate $= \dfrac{12}{11,337} \times 1000 = 1.06$ per 1000 person-months.

Uses of frequency measures

As you may have noted, prevalence and incidence are closely related. However, each measure provides slightly different information. Prevalence is a useful measure in a health care setting, where it is important to assess the public health impact of a specific disease within a community, and to estimate what services are required. However, it is not a measure that can be used to investigate causal relationships. This is because it is not possible to distinguish between the factors that lead to the disease and the factors that cause the disease to persist in that population. Incidence is therefore a more useful measure in this respect, and the ways in which incidence measures can be used to investigate association are outlined in the next chapter.

Crude and specific rates

Incidence measures can also be used to make comparisons of disease (morbidity) or death (mortality) between populations, or in the same population over different time periods. Where an incidence rate applies to an entire population, it is referred to as a *crude* rate. However, care needs to be taken when using crude rates to make comparisons between populations, or over time, because they do not take into account differences in the demographic characteristics (e.g. age, sex, social class, ethnic group) between those populations.

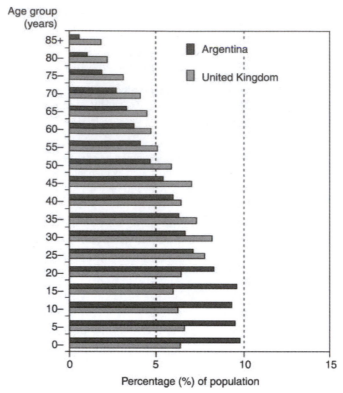

Figure 2.4 Age structure of Argentina and United Kingdom, 1996
Source: data from WHO IARC (2004)

For this reason, *specific* rates are often used, where the rates are reported separately for different categories of people. One of the most important categories is age, since age is strongly associated with the occurrence of disease or death, and can also differ substantially between populations. For example, the crude annual rates of cancer in 1996 in Argentina and the United Kingdom were 145 cases per 100,000 population and 266 cases per 100,000 population, respectively. However, Table 2.1 shows that the age-specific cancer rates for these two populations do not seem to differ markedly. This is where it becomes important to understand what is happening in the two populations with regard to their age demographics. Figure 2.4 shows the population percentages in each 5-year age band. From the figure, it is clear that proportion of the population aged less than 25 years is much larger in Argentina than it is in the United Kingdom. This age group also has the lowest rates of cancer, which is why the crude rate in Argentina seems so much lower than the rate in the United Kingdom.

Standardized rates

Age-specific rates may be more accurate than crude rates, but comparison of many rates over many age bands can be awkward. Even with the age-specific cancer rates

Table 2.1 Crude and age-specific annual rates of cancer in Argentina and the United Kingdom per 100,000 population, 1996.

Age (years)	Argentina	United Kingdom
0–4	4.8	3.2
5–9	3.7	3.1
10–14	4.0	2.8
15–19	5.5	4.3
20–24	6.6	6.1
25–29	10.9	7.8
30–34	20.0	13.7
35–39	36.4	28.4
40–44	65.8	54.3
45–49	118.7	101.1
50–54	198.8	187.0
55–59	305.3	315.1
60–64	445.6	494.8
65–69	611.2	774.8
70–74	815.2	1 122.5
75–79	1 030.3	1 415.5
80–84	1 498.1	1 756.0
85+	2 307.9	1 985.8
All ages (crude rate)	145.0	265.7

Source: data from WHO IARC (2004)

given in Table 2.1, it is still almost impossible to tell which country has the lower annual mortality from cancer. Before reading on, see if you can guess from the information in Table 2.1 which country has the lower mortality.

To make comparisons between rates, some form of standardization needs to be used, so that the demographic characteristics (usually the age structure) of the two populations can be taken into account. Comparing crude rates can be misleading due to the *confounding* effect of age or sex. (Confounding is dealt with in more detail in Chapter 9.)

Standardization is carried out by comparing the population of interest to a 'standard population' for which the age structure (population numbers in each age band) and age-specific rates are known. This can be any population, for example, a larger population of which the population of interest is a part, the combination of two populations that are being compared, or simply another population chosen by the investigator.

Direct standardization

Direct standardization can be carried out when the age-specific rates of the population under study are known. The age structure of the standard population is then applied to these specific rates to obtain a standardized rate. This can be illustrated by standardizing the 1996 Argentina cancer mortality rate to the 1996 UK rate. This is done by multiplying each age-specific rate for the Argentinian population by the number of people in each age band of the standard population (Table 2.2). These numbers are then added together to give the number of cases that would be expected if the study bore the same age distribution as the standard population.

Table 2.2 Direct standardization of Argentinian cancer mortality, using the United Kingdom as standard population

Age (years)	UK (standard) population (× 1000)	UK age-specific rate*	Number of cases	Argentina age-specific rate*	Expected number of cases
0–4	3 575.20	3.2	114	4.8	172
5–9	3 862.70	3.1	120	3.7	143
10–14	3 884.50	2.8	109	4.0	155
15–19	3 682.70	4.3	158	5.5	203
20–24	3 563.90	6.1	217	6.6	235
25–29	4 153.10	7.8	324	10.9	453
30–34	4 745.60	13.7	650	20.0	949
35–39	4 835.30	28.4	1 373	36.4	1 760
40–44	4 169.60	54.3	2 264	65.8	2 744
45–49	3 773.80	101.1	3 815	118.7	4 480
50–54	4 058.90	187.0	7 590	198.8	8 069
55–59	3 250.20	315.1	10 241	305.3	9 923
60–64	2 883.50	494.8	14 268	445.6	12 849
65–69	2 582.60	774.8	20 010	611.2	15 785
70–74	2 334.60	1 122.5	26 206	815.2	19 032
75–79	1 992.70	1 415.5	28 207	1 030.3	20 531
80–84	1 244.30	1 756.0	21 850	1 498.1	18 641
85+	1 162.40	1 985.8	23 083	2 307.9	26 827
All ages	59 755.60		160 600		142 949
Standardized rate*	$\dfrac{160\ 600}{59\ 755\ 600} \times 100\ 000 = 268.8$		$\dfrac{142\ 949}{59\ 755\ 600} \times 100\ 000 = 239.2$		

*per 100 000 population.

Source: data from WHO IARC (2004)

The overall rate can then be calculated by dividing this total number of expected cases by the total number of people in the standard population.

If the United Kingdom 1996 population is used as the standard population, a standardized cancer mortality rate of 239.2 cases per 100,000 is calculated for Argentina in 1996 (Table 2.2). This is clearly lower than the mortality rate for the United Kingdom of 268.8 cases per 100,000. However, it is important to remember that this standardized rate is not a *true* rate, and only tells you how the mortality relates to another population.

Indirect standardization

If the age-specific rates for a population are unknown, or if the population under study is small, then indirect standardization can be used. This method applies the age-specific rates from the standard population to the age structure of the population under study. The standardized rate that is obtained is the rate that would have been expected if the population studied had the same age-specific rates as the standard population. This rate can then be compared with the crude rate for the population under study.

The usual way to present the results of indirect standardization is to calculate the standardized mortality ratio (SMR), which is obtained by dividing the observed crude rate by the expected rate, and multiplying it by 100. More details on SMRs and standardization are given in Activity 2.3.

The next activity will allow you to consolidate what you have learned about crude and specific rates.

Activity 2.2

A total of 1,676,453 deaths (all causes in the whole population) were reported in country X in 2003. The mid-year population in 2003 was estimated to be 198,812,000. HIV-related deaths and mid-year population by age group are given in Table 2.3.

Table 2.3 HIV-related deaths and estimated population by age groups in country X, 2003

Age group (years)	HIV-related deaths	Mid-year population	Age-specific HIV-related death rate (per 100 000 population)
0–4	110	11 217 000	1.0
5–14	30	28 146 000	
15–24	423	31 698 000	1.3
25–34	4 328	37 315 000	11.6
35–44	4 096	29 305 000	
45–54	1 522	19 276 000	7.9
55+	897	41 855 000	2.1
Total	11 406	198 812 000	

1 Calculate the crude death rate (from all causes) in country X in 2003.

Now complete Table 2.3 by answering the following questions:

2 Calculate the crude HIV-related death rate in country X in 2003 in the whole population.

3 Calculate the age-specific HIV-related death rate among 5–14-year-olds and among 35–44-year-olds.

HIV-related deaths and mid-year population by age group in Country Y in 2003 are given in Table 2.4.

4 Calculate the age-specific HIV-related death rates for country Y in 2003, and complete Table 2.4.

The HIV-specific death rate for country Y in 2003 was 4.5 per 100,000 population. Your calculation for Question 2 should have given you the HIV-specific death rate in country X in 2003 as 5.7 per 100,000 population.

5 Can you conclude that a person living in country X has a risk of dying from HIV that is 1.2 times (5.7/4.5 = 1.2) as high as a person living in country Y?

6 Discuss the limitations of the comparison in Question 5 and outline two ways to overcome them.

Table 2.4 HIV-related deaths and estimated population by age group in country Y, 2003

Age group (years)	HIV-related deaths	Mid-year population	Age-specific HIV-related death rate (per 100 000 population)
0–4	336	33 600 000	
5–14	87	62 400 000	
15–24	499	38 400 000	
25–34	4 454	38 400 000	
35–44	3 360	24 000 000	
45–54	1 516	19 200 000	
55+	504	24 000 000	
Total	10 756	240 000 000	4.5

 Feedback

1 Total number of deaths (country X) = 1,676,453.

Mid-year population (country X, 2003) = 198,812,000.

Crude death rate = 1,676,453/198,812,000 × 100 000 = 843 deaths per 100,000 population.

2 Total number of HIV-related deaths = 11,406

Mid-year population = 198,812,000.

Crude HIV-related death rate = 11,406/198,812,000 × 100,000 = 5.7 deaths per 100,000 population.

3 Total number of HIV-related deaths in 5–14-year-olds = 30.

Mid-year population = 28,146,000

Age-specific HIV-related death rate = 30/28,146,000 × 100,000 = 0.11 deaths per 100,000 people aged 5–14 years.

Total number of HIV-related deaths in 35–44-year-olds = 4096.

Mid-year population = 29,305,000

Age-specific HIV-related death rate = 4096/29,305,000 × 100 000 = 14.0 deaths per 100,000 people aged 35–44 years.

4 Age-specific HIV-related death rate for 0–4-year-olds in country Y = 1.0 per 100,000.

Age-specific HIV-related death rate for 5–14-year-olds in country Y = 0.14 per 100,000.

Age-specific HIV-related death rate for 15–24-year-olds in country Y = 1.3 per 100,000.

Age-specific HIV-related death rate for 25–34-year-olds in country Y = 11.6 per 100,000.

Age-specific HIV-related death rate for 35–44-year-olds in country Y = 14.0 per 100,000.

Age-specific HIV-related death rate for 45–54-year-olds in country Y = 7.9 per 100,000.

Age-specific HIV-related death rate for 55-year-olds in country Y = 2.1 per 100,000.

5 It is not possible to conclude that the mortality rate from HIV is 1.2 as high in country X as in country Y for the following reasons:

a) The age-specific HIV-related death rates vary between age groups (from 0.14 per 100,000 in 5–14-year-olds to 14 per 100,000 in 35–44-year-olds).
b) The distribution of the population between age groups differs between country X and country Y. The number of individuals and the proportion of each age group in these two populations are shown in Table 2.5.

Table 2.5 Distribution of age groups in the populations of country X and country Y

Age group (years)	Number of individuals in country X population	%	Number of individuals in country Y population	%
0–4	11 217 000	6	33 600 000	14
5–14	28 146 000	14	62 400 000	26
15–24	31 698 000	16	38 400 000	16
25–34	37 315 000	19	38 400 000	16
35–44	29 305 000	15	24 000 000	10
45–54	19 276 000	10	19 200 000	8
55+	41 855 000	21	24 000 000	10
Total	198 812 000	100	240 000 000	100

6 The comparison of HIV-related death rates is a comparison of crude rates because they are not age-specific. The main limitation of comparing two crude death rates is that no account is taken of the effect of age differences between the two populations. There are two options for overcoming this limitation.

a) You can compare the age-specific HIV-related death rates in the two countries (Table 2.6). This demonstrates no difference in the age-specific HIV-related death rates. However, there are more HIV-related deaths in country X because there are more people in the age groups associated with higher risk of HIV-related death (25–34 years and 35–44 years) in country X than in country Y (Table 2.5).
b) You can adjust for the effect of age on mortality by calculating age-adjusted or standardized HIV-related death rates. Both types of standardization method, direct and indirect, can be applied in this case since the age-specific death rates in both populations are available.

Table 2.6 Age-specific HIV-related death rates in country X and country Y

Age group (years)	Age-specific HIV-related death rate per 100 000 in country X	Age-specific HIV-related death rate per 100 000 in country Y
0–4	1.0	1.0
5–14	0.11	0.14
15–24	1.3	1.3
25–34	11.6	11.6
35–44	14.0	14.0
45–54	7.9	7.9
55+	2.1	2.1

You are not expected to know how to apply the methods of standardization at this stage. However, you do have to know why these methods are applied when comparing mortality and morbidity rates or risks between populations.

If the HIV-related death rate of country Y is adjusted using the population of country X (direct method), the age-adjusted rate for country Y is 5.7 per 100,000 – exactly the same as the rate in country X. This shows that the difference between the unadjusted rates of HIV-related death (5.7 vs. 4.5 per 100,000) is due to the effect of age and can be controlled by standardization.

Activity 2.3

We can look at some data comparing mortality in two populations to illustrate the potential to mislead if only crude measures are used. Look at the data in Table 2.7. We can see that the crude death rate (for all ages in the population) is higher in city A than in city B. If we look at age-specific death rates, we can see that they are higher in each age group category in city B and so, overall, the risk of death is higher in city B. Overall mortality is higher in city A as its population is older (11.0% of the population in city A is 60+ and over, while in city B it is only 4.6%) and, generally, the elderly are at greater risk of dying. In this example we can see that age is acting as a confounder since it is associated with living in City A or B and independently affects the risk of dying.

Table 2.7 Death rates by age in two cities

| Age | City A | | | City B | | |
	No. of deaths	Population (000s)	Death rate (per 1000)	No. of deaths	Population (000s)	Death rate (per 1000)
0–17	2 343	2 101	1.1	2 076	440	4.7
18–44	6 104	2 365	2.6	766	256	3.0
45–60	23 845	857	27.8	3 210	96	33.4
60+	38 102	656	58.1	2 311	38	60.8
All	70 394	5 979	11.8	8 363	830	10.1

We can use statistical techniques to calculate a summary measure, which quantifies the difference in mortality between people living in cities A and B. A summary measure, the SMR, can be derived from the data in Table 2.7. SMRs are often used when presenting routine data and compare the rate of death seen in a study population with a rate seen in a 'standard' population. The word 'standardized' in this context tells us that an adjustment has been made which takes into account the effects of confounding factors – in this case age. You have already come across this indirect method of standardization to calculate SMRs.

1 If we assume that the population of city A is the standard population, calculate the number of deaths we would have expected to see in City B.

2 Once you have done this, calculate the SMR.

Feedback

First construct a table and calculate the number of deaths we would expect to see in city B if the population had similar death rates to our standard population in city A (see Table 2.8).

Table 2.8 Observed and expected death rate

	City A	City B		
Age	Death rate (per 1000)	No. of deaths observed	Population (000s)	No. of deaths expected (per 1000)
0–17	1.1	2 076	440	(440 000 × 1.1)/1000 = 484
18–44	2.6	766	256	(256 000 × 2.6)/1000 = 666
45–60	27.8	3 210	96	(96 000 × 27.8)/1000 = 2 669
60+	58.1	2 311	38	(38 000 × 58.1)/1000 = 2 208
All	11.8	8 363	830	6 027

Once you have calculated the expected deaths, you can calculate the SMR:

$$SMR = \frac{\text{Observed deaths}}{\text{Expected deaths}} (\times 100) = \frac{8363}{6027} \times 100\% = 138.8\%.$$

An SMR of 230% tells us that the population of city B is 1.39 times as likely to die as the population of city A.

Summary

You should be able to define and calculate prevalence and incidence (risk, odds and rate). You should also be able to explain the need for standardization of age when comparing mortality rates. Finally, you should be able to calculate SMR's using indirect standardization.

Reference

WHO IARC (2004) WHO cancer mortality data. Available from http://www-depdb.iarc.fr/who/

3 | Epidemiological measures of health and disease: association and impact

Overview

In epidemiological research, the occurrence of disease in a group of people exposed to a risk factor is compared to that observed in an unexposed group in order to establish causal relationships, and to identify effective interventions. In this way we can quantify the association between a risk (or protective) factor and a disease (or other outcome).

An important application of epidemiology is to estimate how much disease is caused by a certain modifiable risk factor. The data on the impact of risk factors or interventions are essential to assess the effectiveness and cost-effectiveness of interventions. In this chapter, you will learn about epidemiological measures used to quantify the association between a risk (or protective) factor and an outcome, and the measures used to assess the impact of a risk factor or interventions in the population.

Learning objectives

After working through this chapter, you will be better able to:

- **define, calculate and understand the application of measures of association between risk factors and disease based on the ratio of measures of frequency (risk ratio, rate ratio, and odds ratio)**
- **define, calculate and understand the application of measures of association between risk factors and disease based on the difference between measures of frequency (risk difference and rate difference)**
- **select an appropriate measure for different situations and objectives**
- **define and calculate other measures of impact (attributable risk per cent and population attributable risk)**

Key terms

Absolute (attributable) risk A measure of association indicating on an absolute scale how much greater the frequency of diseases is in an exposed group than in an unexposed group, assuming the association between the exposure and disease is causal.

Relative risk Relative measure of risk estimating the magnitude of association between an exposure and disease (or other outcome) indicating the likelihood of developing the disease in those exposed relative to those unexposed

Risk factor Patient characteristic (either inherited, such as a blood group, or behavioural, such as smoking and diet habits) or environmental factor (such as exposure to asbestos) associated with an increased or decreased probability (risk) of developing a disease (or other outcome).

Measures of exposure effect and impact

In the previous chapter, you learned how to calculate the frequency of death or disease (or other health outcome). In this chapter, you will learn how these measures can be used to investigate the *association* between the exposure to a particular risk factor and the occurrence of an outcome of interest (e.g. disease, injury or death). In a descriptive study, we might be interested to find out the proportion of a population that has a particular disease. Once we start to look for links between the disease and other factors, the study becomes analytical in nature (see Figure 3.1).

To investigate a possible association between a risk factor and a particular disease, the incidence of disease in the people exposed to the risk factor is compared with the incidence in a group of people who were not exposed. This comparison can be calculated by various methods, which will be outlined below.

Relative measures

Relative measures estimate the *size* of an association between exposure and disease, and indicate how much more likely people in an exposed group are to develop the disease than those in an unexposed group. In the previous chapter, you learned that there are three ways to measure incidence of disease or incidence of exposure: risk, rate, and odds. There are also three relative measures that can be used to calculate association between disease and exposure: risk ratio, rate ratio and odds ratio.

Risk ratio

The *risk ratio*, also commonly referred to as relative risk (see the note at the end of this discussion of relative measures) is calculated as the ratio between the cumulative incidence in the exposed group and the cumulative incidence in the unexposed group.

However, before we look at the equation for the risk ratio, it is helpful to look at the data we are going to use for any calculations in the form of a 2 × 2 table (Table 3.1). From the information in Table 3.1, and assuming that the data collected were new cases of disease over the course of a year, what is the incidence of disease in this population? See if you can work it out before reading on.

Table 3.1 2 × 2 table

		Disease		
		Yes	No	Total
Risk factor	Exposed	a	b	$a + b$
	Unexposed	c	d	$c + d$
	Total	$a + c$	$b + d$	$a + b + c + d$

The incidence of disease in the entire population is $(a + c)/(a + b + c + d)$ per year. We define the risk ratio as:

$$\text{Risk ratio} = \frac{\text{Risk (cumulative incidence) in the exposed group}}{\text{Risk (cumulative incidence) in the unexposed group}}.$$

Since the incidence of disease in the exposed group is $a/(a + b)$ and in the unexposed group is $c/(c + d)$, the risk ratio can be calculated as:

$$\text{Risk ratio} = \frac{a/(a + b)}{c/(c + d)}.$$

The risk ratio is used as a measure of aetiological strength (i.e. the strength of association between risk factor and outcome). A value of 1.0 will be obtained if the incidence of disease in the exposed and unexposed groups is identical, and therefore indicates that there is no observed association between the exposure and the disease, according to the given data. A value greater than 1.0 indicates a positive association or an increased risk among those exposed to the factor. A value less than 1.0 means that there is an inverse association or a decreased risk among those exposed, or in other words, the exposure is protective.

Rate ratio

The *rate ratio* is calculated in the same way as the risk ratio, except that the incidence rates in the exposed and unexposed groups are used:

$$\text{Rate ratio} = \frac{\text{Incidence rate in the exposed group}}{\text{Incidence rate in the unexposed group}}.$$

The rate ratio takes into account the amount of time that each person contributes to the study, and is therefore preferred in analytical studies in which the outcome is common, and in which large numbers of people are entering and leaving the study population or have changing levels of exposure.

For example, we might be interested to find out whether miners are at higher risk of tuberculosis than men who do not work as miners. In this case, we would compare the incidence rate of tuberculosis in miners (exposed group) with the incidence rate in non-miners (unexposed group). Since the miners will have worked for different lengths of time, the number of person-years at risk can be taken into account. If the incidence rate for miners is 3 cases of tuberculosis per 100 person-years and the rate for non-miners is 0.6 cases of tuberculosis per 100 person-years, the rate ratio is given by comparing the two rates as follows:

$$\text{Rate ratio} = \frac{3 \text{ per 100 person-years}}{0.6 \text{ per 100 person-years}} = 5.0.$$

This shows us that the incidence of tuberculosis was five times as high in miners as in non-miners.

Odds ratio

The *odds ratio* is calculated in a similar way to the risk ratio and the rate ratio, in that the odds in the exposed group are compared with the odds in the unexposed group:

$$\text{Odds ratio} = \frac{\text{Odds of disease in the exposed group}}{\text{Odds of disease in the unexposed group}}.$$

If we use the information from Table 3.1, the odds of disease are the population is calculated as $(a + c)/(b + d)$. The odds of disease in the exposed group are a/b and in the unexposed group are c/d, therefore the odds ratio is:

$$\text{Odds ratio} = \frac{a/b}{c/d}.$$

This equation can be simplified by multiplying the top and bottom parts by bd to give:

$$\text{Odds ratio} = \frac{ad}{cb}.$$

Odds ratios are usually used in studies where the incidence of the disease of interest is not known or if the study participants are selected on the basis of their disease status rather than because of their exposure status. In this case, rather than calculating the odds of disease in the exposed and unexposed groups, the odds of exposure are calculated in those with and without disease. This is known as a case–control study, and you will learn more about this study design in Chapter 7.

Now it is time for you to calculate the risk ratio, rate ratio, and odds ratio for yourself.

Activity 3.1

A study followed a population of 2000 women aged over 65 years for 10 years and measured the number of cases of osteoporosis diagnosed during that time period. The investigators were interested in the effect of regular exercise on the development of osteoporosis and divided the women into two groups: 1000 women who took regular exercise (exposed) and 1000 women who did not take regular exercise (unexposed).

The investigators recorded 800 new cases of osteoporosis over the 10 years of the study, 300 in those who took regular exercise and 500 in those who did not. The number of person-years at risk was 8350 in the exposed group and 6950 in the unexposed group.

1   Calculate the risk ratio, odds ratio and rate ratio for the effect of regular exercise on osteoporosis in these women.

The investigators then decided to do another study to look at osteoporosis in women aged less than 55 years. Again they followed 1000 women who took regular exercise and 1000 women who did not for 10 years. This time they recorded 3 cases of osteoporosis in those who took exercise and 5 cases in those who did not. The number of person-years at risk was 9500 in the exposed group and 9000 in the unexposed group.

2   Calculate the risk ratio, odds ratio and rate ratio for the effect of regular exercise on osteoporosis in these younger women.

 Feedback

1 To calculate the risk ratio, first work out the incidence of osteoporosis in the older women who took exercise and in those who did not:

Incidence in women who took regular exercise = 300 / 1000 = 0.3 per 10 years.
Incidence in women who took no regular exercise = 500 / 1000 = 0.5 per 10 years.
Then divide the incidence in the exposed group by the incidence in the unexposed group:

$$\text{Risk ratio} = \frac{0.3 \text{ per } 10 \text{ years}}{0.5 \text{ per } 10 \text{ years}} = 0.6.$$

This indicates that women aged over 65 years who take regular exercise have a 40% lower risk of developing osteoporosis than women who do not take regular exercise.

To calculate the odds ratio, work out the odds of osteoporosis in women who took exercise and in those who did not take regular exercise:

Odds in women who took regular exercise over 10 years = 300/(1000 − 300) = 300/700 = 0.43.

Odds in women who took no regular exercise over 10 years = 500/(1000 − 500) = 500/500 = 1.

Odds ratio = 0.43 / 1.0 = 0.43.

Therefore, women aged over 65 years who take regular exercise have a 57% lower odds of developing osteoporosis than women who do not take regular exercise.

To calculate the rate ratio, work out the rate of osteoporosis in women who took exercise and in those who did not take regular exercise:

Rate in women who took regular exercise = 300 / 8350 person-years = 0.036 per person-year = 3.6 per 100 person-years.

Rate in women who did not take regular exercise = 500 / 6950 person-years = 0.072 per person-year = 7.2 per 100 person-years.

$$\text{Rate ratio} = \frac{3.6 \text{ per } 100 \text{ person-years}}{7.2 \text{ per } 100 \text{ person-years}} = 0.5.$$

Therefore, women aged over 65 years who take regular exercise have a 50% lower rate of osteoporosis than women who do not take regular exercise.

In this case, the rate ratio is probably the most appropriate measure since it takes into account the person-years at risk in the exposed and unexposed groups.

2 Now for the calculations in younger women, starting with the risk ratio:

Incidence in women who took regular exercise = 3/1000 = 0.003 per 10 years.

Incidence in women who took no regular exercise = 5/1000 = 0.005 per 10 years.

Then divide the incidence in the exposed group by the incidence in the unexposed group:

$$\text{Risk ratio} = \frac{0.003 \text{ per 10 years}}{0.005 \text{ per 10 years}} = 0.6.$$

This indicates that women aged less than 55 years who take regular exercise have a 40% lower risk of developing osteoporosis than women who do not take regular exercise. Note that this is the same as the answer you got in Question 1.

To calculate the odds ratio, work out the odds of osteoporosis in women who took exercise and in those who did not take regular exercise:

Odds in women who took regular exercise over 10 years = 3/(1000 − 3) = 3/997 = 0.003.

Odds in women who took no regular exercise over 10 years = 5/(1000 − 5) = 5/995 = 0.005.

Odds ratio = 0.003 / 0.005 = 0.6.

Therefore, women aged less than 55 years who take regular exercise have a 40% lower odds of developing osteoporosis than women who do not take regular exercise.
Note how similar this odds ratio is to the risk ratio you calculated above.

To calculate the rate ratio, work out the rate of osteoporosis in women who took exercise and in those who did not take regular exercise:

Rate in women who took regular exercise = 3/9500 person-years = 0.00032 per person-year = 3.2 per 10,000 person-years.

Rate in women who did not take regular exercise = 5/9000 person-years = 0.00056 per person-year = 5.6 per 10,000 person-years.

$$\text{Rate ratio} = \frac{3.2 \text{ per 10,000 person-years}}{5.6 \text{ per 10,000 person-years}} = 0.57.$$

Therefore, women aged less than 55 years who take regular exercise have a 43% lower rate of developing osteoporosis than women who do not take regular exercise.

Note how similar all three measures now are to one another.

In Activity 3.1, the measures of effect in Question 2 gave similar estimates for the risk ratio, rate ratio and odds ratio. This is because the outcome of interest was rare. The number of women at risk remained largely constant throughout the study because the cases represented a very small proportion of the population. In practice, these three measures of effect will only yield similar estimates if the disease or condition is rare (e.g. most cancers, congenital malformations). For common diseases (e.g. most infectious disease), the estimates obtained may differ substantially.

Note that the term *relative risk* is often used to refer collectively to the three ratios outlined above. It is important to remember this when reading studies that quote a 'relative risk' measurement, since a risk ratio may be very different from an odds ratio, especially if the disease or exposure is common.

Absolute measures

Relative measures are useful when we want to know how strongly an exposure is associated with a particular disease, but they do not give us any indication of the impact of that exposure on the incidence of disease in that population. This has important implications for any public health prevention measures we may want to take.

Absolute measures are therefore used to indicate exactly what impact a particular disease or condition will have on a population, in terms of the numbers or percentage of that population affected by their being exposed. For example, the risk of cancer in people exposed to a certain carcinogen may be 20 times that observed in people not exposed. However, this tells us nothing about how common that type of cancer might be; therefore, in absolute terms, the number of people affected in the exposed group might still be relatively small. The absolute or attributable risk will tell us exactly how many more people are affected in the exposed group than in the unexposed group, and is arguably a more useful measure in public health terms.

Attributable (absolute) risk

The *attributable* or *absolute risk* can give information on how much greater the frequency of a disease is in the exposed group than in the unexposed group, assuming the association between the exposure and disease is causal.

Attributable risk measures the *difference* in frequency of a disease between two groups, not the magnitude of association between the risk factor and the outcome (as in a relative risk). It is the risk of disease in the exposed group that is *attributable* to the risk factor, after taking into account the underlying level of disease in the population (from other causes). Attributable risk is also known as risk difference or excess risk.

Attributable risk = Incidence in exposed group – Incidence in non-exposed group.

For example, if we know that the risk of disease in those exposed is 5 cases per 1000 people per year and in those unexposed is 3 cases per 1000 people per year, the risk that is attributable to the exposure (i.e. the attributable risk) is 2 cases per 1000 people per year.

This can be expressed as the proportion of disease in the exposed group attributable to the exposure (the proportion of *additional* cases). This is known as the attributable risk per cent of the aetiologic fraction.

$$\textbf{Attributable risk per cent} = \frac{\text{Incidence in exposed group} - \text{Incidence in non-exposed group}}{\text{Incidence in exposed group}}.$$

In our example, the attributable fraction will be the attributable risk we have calculated above (2 per 1000 per year) divided by the risk in the exposed group (5 per 1000 per year), which gives an attributable fraction of 0.4. If we multiply this by 100, we get an attributable risk of 40%. This means that 40% of disease cases could have been prevented if the exposed group had not been exposed to the risk factor.

The attributable fraction can also be calculated from the relative risk (risk ratio or rate ratio) by using the following formula, which is useful if we do not know the incidence of disease in the exposed and unexposed groups:

$$\text{Attributable fraction} = \frac{\text{Risk (or rate) ratio} - 1}{\text{Risk (or rate) ratio}}.$$

In our example, if we knew only that the risk ratio was 1.67, and did not know the risks in the exposed and unexposed groups, we could use the above formula to give an attributable fraction of 0.4, as before.

The attributable fraction is usually used if there is a positive association between the exposure and the outcome (i.e. the risk or rate ratio is greater than 1). However, if the exposure prevents the outcome, as in our example of the effect of regular exercise on osteoporosis, the attributable fraction will be negative, which is difficult to interpret. In such a case, we would look instead at the risk or rate that is attributed to not being exposed by replacing the denominator by the risk in the unexposed group. This measure is known as the *preventable fraction* in the non-exposed group:

$$\text{Preventable fraction} = \frac{\text{Risk in unexposed group} - \text{Risk in exposed group}}{\text{Risk in unexposed group}}.$$

This formula can also be expressed in terms of the risk or rate ratio, as follows:

Preventable fraction = 1 − Risk (or rate) ratio.

Population attributable (absolute) risk

The same concept can be applied to the population as a whole. It is of benefit to public health if we can estimate the excess disease present in a population that is due to a particular risk factor, or estimate the relative importance of different risk factors.

Population attributable risk = Incidence in the *whole* population − Incidence in non-exposed population.

The population attributable risk fraction is the proportion of disease observed in the whole population that is attributable to exposure to the risk factor. It estimates the proportion of disease that might be prevented if the risk factor were removed.

Population attributable risk fraction =
$$\frac{\text{Incidence in the } whole \text{ population} - \text{Incidence in the non-exposed population}}{\text{Incidence in the } whole \text{ population}}.$$

The population attributable risk fraction can be used to estimate the benefit of a proposed intervention, such as the number of lung cancer deaths that could be prevented by introducing a smoking reduction programme in a large population.

Measures of attributable risk rely on a number of assumptions: first, that the association between the risk factor and the outcome is causal; second, that there is no confounding or bias in the measurement of incidence (e.g. selection bias).

If we do not know the risk of disease in the population, we can still calculate the population attributable risk, as long as we know the proportion of the population in the exposed group (p):

Population attributable risk = p × Attributable risk.

The population attributable risk will therefore always be less than the attributable risk in the exposed group, since p should always be less than 1. For example, suppose we know that the rate of liver cancer to be 602 per 100,000 person-years in a group of people with chronic hepatitis B infection and 4 per 100,000 person-years in those without chronic hepatitis B infection. If the rate of liver cancer in the entire population is 94 per 100,000 person-years, the population attributable risk is $(94 - 4) = 90$ per 100,000 person-years.

Population attributable fraction

Finally, we can indicate what proportion of the total risk of the disease in the population is associated with the exposure. This is expressed as the population attributable fraction (or the population attributable risk per cent, if multiplied by 100), and indicates the proportion of the disease in the population that could be prevented if exposure to the risk factor could be eliminated, and the entire population was unexposed.

This is calculated in a similar way to the attributable fraction:

$$\text{Population attributable fraction} = \frac{\text{Population attributable risk}}{\text{Risk of disease in population}}.$$

In our previous example of the impact of chronic hepatitis B infection on the rate of liver cancer, the rate of liver cancer in the population was 94 per 100,000 person-years, and the population attributable risk was 90 per 100,000 person-years. Therefore we calculate the population attributable fraction (given by 90 divided by 94), which gives a value of 0.96. This means that, if we could prevent chronic hepatitis B infection in this population, we estimate that 96% of cases of liver cancer could be prevented.

An example

The following is a hypothetical example to illustrate the use of attributable risk. A causal association has been established between standing and backache. Imagine we wanted to establish how important standing was as a risk factor for backache in relation to all cases of backache. The risk of backache per 100 female workers over a 2-year period in standing female workers is 12.3 and for other female workers it is 7.7. The risk of backache in all female workers is 8.3.

We assume that while women who stood while working had a risk of backache of 12.3 per 100 persons over a 2-year period, these women would have the same risk as other female workers (who do not stand at work) of 7.7 if they did not stand at work.

The attributable risk resulting from standing at work is $12.3 - 7.7 = 4.6$ over a 2-year period. That is, 37.4% of the risk of backache in women standing at work over 2 years can be attributed to their standing at work.

The risk of backache in all women would have been 7.7 per 100 persons over 2 years (and not 8.3) if nobody had been standing at work. The risk of backache related to standing at work, the population attributable risk, is $8.3 - 7.7 = 0.6$ per 100 persons over 2 years.

To calculate how important standing is as a risk factor for backache in the whole population of working women we can express it as a percentage, the population attributable per cent: (8.3–7.7)/8.3 = 7%. Which means that in all female workers the proportion of risk of backache which results from standing at work is 7%.

In this example we are assuming that the relationship between standing and backache is casual; and that there is no selection bias (e.g. those recruited to standing jobs are at no greater risk of backache prior to the job) or confounding (e.g. that those recruited to standing jobs are older).

Caution is needed when extrapolating data from one population to another as both levels of exposure and underlying susceptibility may be different within and between populations.

Selection of appropriate measure for different study designs

You have now learned how frequency and association, effect and impact can be measured. In this section, you will find out which types of study design are needed to obtain these measures.

The main types of epidemiological study designs are summarized in Figure 3.1. Below is a brief description of each study type and the measures that are associated with them. Further details of all these study types will be provided in the next four chapters.

Cross-sectional studies

A *cross-sectional study* is a survey of a population at a single point in time. This type of study has the advantage of being fairly quick and easy to perform. Cross-sectional studies can be used to determine the prevalence of risk factors and disease in a defined population. They can also be used to measure associations between diseases and risk factors, by means of the prevalence ratio. However, because they are carried out at a single point in time, they are unsuitable for making causal hypotheses between diseases and risk factors (Chapter 4).

Ecological studies

In an *ecological study*, the units of analysis are populations or groups of people rather than individuals. Although these types of study can generate useful topics for further research, like cross-sectional studies they are unlikely to establish a causal relationship between an exposure and an outcome. Ecological studies can be either cross-sectional or longitudinal in nature. Longitudinal studies give more indication of temporal relationships, but because populations and not individuals are under study, individual cohort and case–control studies are needed to establish possible causal relationships at the individual level (Chapter 5).

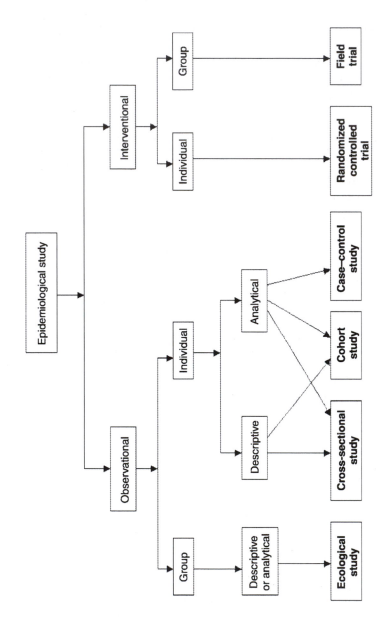

Figure 3.1 Main types of epidemiological study designs

Cohort study

In a *cohort study*, participants are followed over time to see whether they develop the disease of interest. Participants are selected on the basis of whether they are exposed to a potential risk factor. All participants should be free of the disease under investigation at the start of the study. In a *prospective* cohort study the investigator assembles the study groups on the basis of exposure to a risk factor, collects baseline data, and continues to collect data on the outcome and other relevant variables over time. In a *retrospective* cohort study, the investigator goes back in time to define the exposed and unexposed groups and reviews medical records to follow participants and review outcomes to the present day. All three measures of relative risk (risk ratio, rate ratio, and odds ratio) can be calculated from cohort studies, since the incidence of disease in the exposed and unexposed groups is known. Cohort studies can also be used to measure standardized mortality ratios and the incidence of disease. They can also be used to measure attributable risk and population attributable risk (Chapter 6).

Case–control study

In a *case–control study*, a group of cases (individuals who have the disease or outcome of interest) and a group of controls (individuals who do not have the disease or outcome of interest) are identified. Then the prevalence of or level of exposure to a risk (or protective) factor is measured and compared between the two groups. Usually, this study design is less time-consuming and less expensive. The design allows the investigation of several risk factors for a given disease at the same time, and the study of rare diseases. However, identifying suitable controls can be difficult, and this design is liable to have selection and measurement biases. In case–control studies, participants are selected on the basis of their disease status and not their exposure status. Therefore, it is not possible to calculate the incidence of disease in the exposed and unexposed individuals. It is, however, possible to calculate the odds of exposure among cases and among controls and obtain an odds ratio of exposure (Chapter 7).

Intervention study

An *intervention study* is an epidemiological experiment in which the investigator randomly allocates selected individuals (or groups of individuals) to an intervention group (the group that receives the intervention under investigation) or to control group (the group that does not receive the intervention). Individuals allocated to both groups must be similar in their background characteristics. The investigator then measures and compares the incidence of the outcome of interest in the two groups. An example of a group-level study is a field trial or a cluster randomized trial, and an example of an individual study is a randomized controlled trial. The main measures of effect obtained from an intervention study are the risk ratio or rate ratio. It is also possible to calculate the attributable risk and the population attributable risk from the results of an intervention study (Chapter 8).

 **Activity 3.2**

This is an extended activity in three parts, each consisting of one or more questions to answer. If you find any question unclear or difficult, refer back to the text above while trying to answer. Try to complete the entire activity before you look at the feedback.

Between 1951 and 1971, a total of 10,000 deaths were recorded among 34,440 male British doctors (Doll and Peto 1976). Of these deaths, 441 were from lung cancer and 3191 were from ischaemic heart disease. Doctors who smoked at least one cigarette per day during this follow-up period were classified as smokers and the rest as non-smokers. The age-adjusted annual death rates per 100,000 male doctors for lung cancer and ischaemic heart disease among smokers and non-smokers are given in Table 3.2.

Table 3.2 Cause of death and specific death rates by smoking habits of British male doctors, 1951–71

Cause of death	Annual death rate per 100 000 doctors	
	Non-smokers	Smokers
Lung cancer	10	140
Ischaemic heart disease	413	669

Source: based on Doll and Peto (1976)

1 Calculate an appropriate epidemiological measure to assess the strength of association between smoking and lung cancer, and smoking and ischaemic heart disease.

   a) Which disease is strongly associated with smoking?
   b) Reduction in mortality from which disease would have greater public health impact if there were a reduction in smoking?
   c) What assumptions did you make when estimating the impact of a reduction in smoking?

2 Assume that the data shown in Table 3.2 are valid and that smoking causes lung cancer.

   a) What percentage of the risk of death from lung cancer is attributable to smoking?
   b) If 50% of doctors stopped smoking, by what percentage would the risk of lung cancer death among the smokers be reduced?

A case–control study was conducted to investigate the risk factors for myocardial infarction (Doll and Peto 1976). Information on smoking was collected from cases and controls. Current cigarette smoking, defined as smoking within the past 3 months, was reported by 60 of the 400 myocardial infarction cases and by 40 of the 400 healthy controls.

3 Set up a 2 × 2 table, and estimate the strength of association between current smoking and myocardial infarction.

The incidence of tuberculosis and the mid-year population of different ethnic groups in a European country, country Z, in 2004 are given in Table 3.3.

Table 3.3 Incidence of tuberculosis and mid-year population by ethnic group in country Z, 2004

Ethnic group	Number of new tuberculosis cases, 2004	Mid-year population, 2004
European	2 890	69 900 000
Indian	1 900	1 790 000
Other	400	1 650 000
Total	5 190	73 340 000

4 Calculate the incidence rate and rate ratio for each group.

 a) Which ethnic group is strongly associated with tuberculosis?
 b) Why is the number of tuberculosis cases greater in the European group even though the incidence rate is lower than in the other two groups?

5 The incidence rate for the entire population is 7.1 per 100,000 person-years. Assume that a targeted intervention has reduced the incidence rate in the Indian and the other ethnic groups to the level of that in the European group (4.1 per 100,000 person-years).

 a) What percentage of tuberculosis cases in the Indian group would be prevented?
 b) What percentage of tuberculosis cases in the whole population would be prevented?

Feedback

1 An appropriate measure to assess the strength of an association is relative risk. In this example the relative risk can be estimated by the rate ratio.

Rate ratio of lung cancer in smokers compared to non-smokers $= \dfrac{140/100,000}{10/100,000} = 14$.

Rate ratio of ischaemic heart disease (IHD) in smokers compared to non-smokers $= \dfrac{669/100,000}{413/100,000} = 1.6$.

 a) Clearly, smoking is more strongly associated with lung cancer than with IHD.
 b) To assess the impact of smoking, the excess mortality attributable to smoking must be estimated:

 Attributable risk of smoking for lung cancer $= (140/100,000) - (10/100,000) = 130/100,000$.

 Attributable risk of smoking for IHD $= (669/100,000) - (413/100,000) = 256/100,000$.

 It would seem that, among smokers, a reduction in smoking would prevent far more deaths from IHD than from lung cancer. The explanation for this is that, among non-smokers, the death rate from lung cancer is fairly low (10/100,000), but the death rate from IHD is 413/100,000. Consequently, the 1.6-fold increase in IHD mortality associated with smoking affects a much larger number of people than the 14-fold increase in the risk of death from lung cancer. Thus, the potential public health impact of reduction in smoking on mortality is far greater for IHD than for lung cancer.

c) To arrive at the conclusions of (b), it is necessary to assume that smoking is causally related to lung cancer and to IHD, and that cessation of smoking will have similar effect on the mortality from each of these diseases.

2 Attributable risk per cent = attributable fraction $\times$ 100

$$= \frac{\text{Risk in the smokers} - \text{Risk in the non-smokers}}{\text{Risk in the smokers}} \times 100.$$

a) So, the risk of death from lung cancer attributable to smoking =

$$\frac{(140/100,000) - (10/100,000)}{(140/100,000)} \times 100 = 93\%.$$

Alternatively, attributable risk can be calculated from the relative risk of lung cancer in smokers compared to non-smokers as follows:

$$\text{Attributable risk per cent} = \frac{\text{Relative risk} - 1}{\text{Relative risk}} \times 100.$$

b) If 50% of doctors stopped smoking, then the attributable risk among the smokers would be reduced by 50%. So, the risk of lung cancer death would be reduced by (93% $\times$ 0.5 =) 46.5% among the smokers.

The percentage reduction in the risk of lung cancer death can also be estimated in the following way:
Lung cancer deaths attributable to smoking = (140/100,000) − (10/100,000) = 130/100,000.
Assuming 50% reduction in smoking = 50% reduction in the attributable risk, then the reduced attributable risk = (130/100,000) $\times$ 0.5 = 65/100,000.
The percentage reduction in the risk of lung cancer death among the smokers = (65/140) $\times$ 100 = 46.5%.

3 Your table should look like Table 3.4. As this is a case–control study, an appropriate measure to assess the strength of association between smoking and myocardial infarction is the odds ratio.

$$\text{Odds ratio} = \frac{60/340}{40/360} = \frac{6 \times 360}{40 \times 340} = 1.6.$$

This shows that the odds of exposure to smoking are 1.6 times higher in cases of myocardial infarction compared to healthy controls.

Table 3.4 Odds of smoking in cases and controls

Risk factor	Cases (n = 400)	Controls (n = 400)
Smokers	60	40
Non-smokers	340	360

4 The incidence rate and rate ratio for tuberculosis in the ethnic groups is given in Table 3.5.

a) The rate ratio is 25.7 times as high in the Indian group as in the European group; for other ethnic groups, the rate ratio is 5.9 times as high as in the European group. Thus, the Indian group is more strongly associated with tuberculosis than are European and other ethnic groups.

Table 3.5 Incidence of tuberculosis, mid-year population and incidence rate by ethnic group in country Z in 2004

Ethnic group	Number of new tuberculosis cases in 2004	Mid-year population in 2004	Incidence rate per 100 000	Rate ratio
European	2 890	69 900 000	4.1	1
Indian	1 900	1 790 000	106.1	25.7
Other	400	1 650 000	24.2	5.9
Total	5 190	73 340 000	7.1	

b) The number of tuberculosis cases is greater in the European group since this group constitutes 95% of the population. Thus, even though the rate is lower in the other two groups, the number of cases is higher in the European group.

5 Assuming that a targeted intervention has reduced the incidence rate in the Indian group to 4.1/100,000:

a) the percentage reduction of tuberculosis cases in the Indian group

$$= \frac{\text{Current rate} - \text{Reduced rate}}{\text{Current rate}} \times 100 = \frac{106.1 - 4.1}{106.1} \times 100 = 96.1\%;$$

b) the percentage reduction of tuberculosis cases in the whole population

$$= \frac{7.1 - 4.1}{7.1} \times 100 = 41.6\%.$$

This means that if the incidence rate in the Indian group were reduced to the level of the European group, then 96.1% of cases of tuberculosis in the Indian population would be prevented. However, only 41.6% of cases in the whole population would be prevented.

Summary

In this chapter you have learned about the measures of association commonly used in epidemiological studies. You should understand the application of the risk ratio, rate ratio and odds ratio. You should understand the application of attributable risk (risk difference and rate difference) and attributable fraction. You should also be able to calculate measures of impact (population attributable risk and population attributable fraction). Finally, you should be able to select an appropriate measure for different study designs. You will learn more about the application and interpretation of measures of association in the next four chapters.

Reference

Doll R, Peto R (1976) Mortality in relation to smoking: 20 years' observation on male British doctors. *British Medical Journal* ii: 1525–36.

4 Cross-sectional studies

Overview

In this chapter you will learn about the features, advantages and limitations of cross-sectional studies. Cross-sectional studies or surveys can be either descriptive or analytical. This kind of study can give information on the frequency and characteristics of a disease by providing a snapshot of the health experience of a specific population at a specific point in time.

Learning objectives

After working through this chapter, you will be better able to:

- **describe the basic features and uses of cross-sectional studies**
- **discuss the potential sources of bias in these study designs**
- **understand the strengths and limitations of cross-sectional studies.**

Key terms

Bias Any error that results in a systematic deviation from the true estimation of the association between exposure and outcome.

Chance The possibility that the results of an epidemiological study are due to chance alone rather than the truth.

What is a cross-sectional study?

In a cross-sectional study, data are collected on each study participant at a single point in time. Cross-sectional studies are sometimes referred to as 'prevalence studies', since they collect data on existing (prevalent) cases of disease. Such a study may take the form of a survey, and could be used to assess the prevalence of tuberculosis in a defined population, for example. This is known as a *descriptive* cross-sectional study. However, it is also possible to investigate associations between the disease and other factors using this study design, and this type of study is described as *analytical*. In practice, cross-sectional studies can be both descriptive and analytical in design (see Figure 3.1).

Descriptive studies

A descriptive cross-sectional study collects information on the frequency and distribution of health-related exposures or outcomes in a defined population. The main epidemiological outcome measure obtained is therefore the prevalence of that outcome. As you will recall from Chapter 2, prevalence can be recorded as either point prevalence or period prevalence, depending on how the investigator asks the question. For example, if participants are asked about their current status with regard to a particular disease or outcome, then a measure of point prevalence will be obtained; if they are asked whether they have had a particular disease within the past month, then the measure is of period prevalence.

Survey questions that give a measure of period prevalence of an outcome are often included to decrease the sample size that is required, since they are more likely to pick up additional cases of disease or events that might otherwise be missed by concentrating on a shorter period of time. However, these questions may also increase the chance of recall bias. This bias is an error in the recalling of past events. The participant may not accurately remember an event taking place, may not have recorded it, or may be unsure exactly when the event did actually occur. Obviously, the longer the recall period, the more chance there is of errors being made.

Most cross-sectional studies include a mixture of questions and measurements on the current (e.g. height, weight, blood pressure, age, sex, behaviours) and past (e.g. vaccinations, other exposures) status of the participants.

Analytical studies

Analytical cross-sectional studies are undertaken to investigate the association between exposure to risk factors and the outcome of interest. They require this information to be collected simultaneously on each individual.

Recall bias is even more relevant in analytical studies as the collection of information on exposure to potential risk factors is retrospective. There are certainly some factors that can be reliably collected retrospectively; however, if a participant was exposed to the risk factor a long time ago, this may involve problems with recall. Bias occurs when there is a systematic difference in the participant's ability to recall accurately past events or experiences that is not independent of the disease/exposure status – for example, a person may be more likely to remember an exposure to a potential risk factor if they have become ill, especially if they are aware there may be a link.

One of the limitations of collecting information on exposure and outcome data simultaneously is that it is not possible to show causality (whether having the putative risk factor for a disease led to developing the disease itself). To have any indication of causal association, the exposure must have occurred before the out-come, and sometimes a long time before. For example, the time between exposure to HIV and onset of AIDS can be more than 10 years, and it may have taken many decades for someone exposed to asbestos dust to develop a mesothelioma.

Whether it is appropriate to collect exposure and outcome data simultaneously depends on the risk factors. If exposure to the risk factor is constant, such as blood group and genetic factors, a current measurement of the exposure to these risk factors can be a good proxy for previous exposure. We do not expect disease status or lifestyle changes to affect these factors. However, risk factors such as diet and lifestyle may change over time, and particularly during illness, which might give a false impression that change in diet caused the illness even though the participant might have changed their diet because they were ill. Other factors, such as exercise levels, may change little over time, and again may be a good proxy for past exposure, particularly because recall of past exercise may be unreliable.

Non-response is a problem for all types of study. People who do not respond (non-responders) or participate in surveys usually have different characteristics from those who do (responders). This can introduce a systematic bias into the prevalence estimates if non-response is associated in some way with the outcome. Many factors can influence the response of potential participants to a study.

Because of these potential information or selection biases (recall and non-response bias), cross-sectional studies can only give an indication of the potential risk factors for a disease and cannot prove causation. Causation must then be confirmed by other, more rigorous studies. For this reason, cross-sectional studies are generally used for generating research questions (hypotheses) and for health service planning, rather than for establishing causal links.

Study design

Sampling

In any study, it is important that the sample population is representative of the general population to which the results of that study will be applied. This can be achieved by drawing a random sample from the study population. If the study is to include a sample of people living in a certain area, then it is important to make sure that groups who are often hard to reach are included, such as the homeless, people in institutions, people who are at work, or people who do not have a telephone.

The sample size must be large enough to give the study enough power to detect a valid estimate, and enough precision for the value estimate of the sample to reflect the true population value. The larger the sample size the less likely the results of a study are due simply to chance alone (this is the power of the study to identify the true value), and less variability around the estimate (this is the precision of a study). However, any increase in the sample size and corresponding increase in power will have implications for how much the study costs and how long it takes. Therefore it is important to establish the minimum (clinically or biologically) significant value one wishes to detect, and the power with which one wishes to detect at least that difference determines sample size. Sample size calculations can be made using computer programs or by consulting sample size tables.

Data collection

In cross-sectional studies, data on exposures and outcomes are collected simul-taneously, so it is important that the investigators have decided on a clear definitions of cases (those with the outcome of interest) and exposures (potential risk factors for that outcome) they are interested in before they start collecting data. Case definition is especially important to ensure that those with the outcome are correctly identified, and specific inclusion and exclusion criteria need to be established – for example, a study may include cases identified in a particular setting and having undergone a specific diagnostic test and may exclude cases on the basis of age or duration of illness.

The methods used to collect the data will depend on the exposures and outcomes being studied and how practical and costly it is to collect them. Many different methods can be used, and data can be obtained from the study participants directly or indirectly.

Direct methods include questionnaires and interviews, which can be carried out face-to-face, by telephone, by post, or even by e-mail. Participants may need to undergo a medical examination or have a blood sample taken for a diagnostic test to determine whether they are a case. The advantage of direct data collection is that it is collected prospectively (even though questions may relate to historical events) and questionnaires are designed with a specific study in mind. However, there may be recall bias (as mentioned) and a poor response rate. Direct data collection can also be costly and time-consuming.

If data for a study are already collected routinely, the investigators may be able to obtain data from indirect sources (e.g. medical records, census data, health surveys, records kept by employers, cancer registries). The advantage of using routine data sources is that the data are already available and can provide a lot of information relatively quickly and cheaply (compared to collecting data from scratch). A disadvantage, however, is that data quality may be poor – there may be missing and inaccurate data. Usually routine data systems are designed to serve objectives such as surveillance, and not a research study, so routine data may not be able to provide all the information required by a study. Therefore a combination of data collection methods may be used. (Routine data are discussed in greater detail in Chapter 11.)

However, whichever methods are used, it is important that the methods of collecting data are standardized, and that the investigators ensure the *validity* of the methods used (i.e. that they really are measuring what they purport to measure).

Analysis

Variables on outcome and exposure status can take several different forms. *Discrete* variables such as *binary* (either/or) variables (e.g. presence or absence of illness or injury, death), and *categorical* variables where more than two options are possible (e.g. ethnic group, categories of levels of smoking) can be presented as proportions. As already mentioned above, the main outcome measure of cross-sectional studies is point or period prevalence such as the proportion of patients with an illness.

Continuous variables, where there are possible values along a continuum within a given range (e.g. height, weight, blood pressure) can be analysed using the mean and standard deviation or the median and interquartile range. For example, it may be appropriate to look at the average measure in a population and compare this with the average in another standard population, while of course remembering the issues discussed in Chapter 2 about stardardized morbidity ratios. It is also possible to dichotomize the variables (split values into two categories) – for example, weight above or below 100 kg, if the question is about the prevalence of overweight people in a population.

In an analytical cross-sectional study, the *prevalence ratio* can be calculated. This is the ratio of the prevalence of the outcome in those exposed to the risk factor under study divided by the prevalence in those who were unexposed (see Chapter 2).

The association between the possible risk factor and the outcome can also be measured by using the odds ratio, as long as exposure to that particular risk factor is aetiologically relevant, or if some measure of past exposure has been obtained. This odds ratio is then the odds ratio of exposure, and when we calculate it we are treating our study as if it were a case–control study (the odds of exposure among the cases compared with the odds of exposure among the controls – see Chapter 7). However, the odds ratio of exposure will only provide a good estimate of the prevalence ratio if the prevalence of the outcome is low (say, less than 15%).

Strengths and weaknesses

Cross-sectional studies have the main advantage of being relatively quick and easy to perform in comparison with cohort studies, for example. They can determine the prevalence of risk factors and the frequency of prevalent cases of disease in a defined population. They are also useful for measuring current health status, which can be used in the planning of health services or the determination of health practices. Repeated studies can be used to determine changes in risk factors and disease frequency in populations.

One main disadvantage of cross-sectional studies is that data on disease and risk factors are collected simultaneously. This poses problems when trying to determine temporal relationships. However, where the exposure status does not change over time (e.g. eye colour or blood group), cross-sectional studies can be used to test hypotheses.

Cross-sectional studies also include prevalent rather than incident cases, which might cause the study group to be biased toward patients with chronic illness, since people with acute fatal illnesses are unlikely to be included if they died before detection by the survey.

✎ Activity 4.1

In the following activity, you will look at a cross-sectional study carried out in Tanzania to investigate the association between insecticide-treated bed nets and the prevalence of malaria in young children.

Many intervention studies have shown that mosquito nets treated with insecticide can reduce the morbidity and mortality from malaria in young children in Africa. However, Abdulla *et al.* (2001) were interested in whether countries that have implemented programmes to supply these treated nets to communities with a high prevalence of malaria have seen the benefits highlighted by the intervention studies. In 1997 the investigators carried out a cross-sectional study of children under 2 years of age in 18 villages in Tanzania at the beginning of a marketing campaign to promote the use of treated nets. They collected data on net ownership and other factors by questionnaire (the mothers of the children were interviewed), and took blood samples from the children in the study to assess whether they were infected with malaria parasites (parasitaemia), and also to see whether they were anaemic (as a consequence). The children were also assessed for clinical signs of malaria. Two further surveys were done over the next 2 years. A different random sample of children was selected on each occasion.

The investigators identified 985 eligible children, and interviewed the mothers of 827 of these children over the course of the three cross-sectional surveys (16 mothers refused consent, and 142 could not be contacted). Of the 827 interviewees, data from 748 were included in the analysis because 68 children were aged over 2 years at the time of sampling and net status was not known for 11 children. Table 4.1 shows some of the results from the study.

Table 4.1 Results of three cross-sectional surveys, 1997–1999

	Year of survey		
	1997	1998	1999
Number of children eligible	325	330	330
Number of children analysed	240	269	239
Number (%) of net ownership			
no net	100 (42%)	49 (18%)	40 (17%)
untreated net	116 (48%)	64 (24%)	53 (22%)
treated net	24 (10%)	156 (58%)	146 (61%)
Number (%) of children			
with anaemia	118 (49%)	83 (31%)	62 (26%)
with parasitaemia	151 (63%)	126 (47%)	90 (38%)
with splenomegaly	207 (86%)	144 (54%)	117 (49%)

Source: data from Abdulla et al. (2001)

Answer the following questions about this study. Refer to the text above if you need help.

1   Is this a descriptive or an analytical cross-sectional study?

2   Does it matter that data from some of the eligible children were not included in the analysis?

3   Describe the results of the study shown in Table 4.1. Can you calculate the effect of net ownership on the proportion of children with malaria parasitaemia from this table?

Table 4.2 shows numbers of children with anaemia and parasitaemia according to net ownership for all three surveys.

4   What is the prevalence ratio for the effect of owning a treated net on the prevalence of anaemia?

5   What is the prevalence ratio for the effect of not owning a net (whether treated or untreated) on the prevalence of parasitaemia?

Table 4.2 Effect of nets on prevalence of anaemia and parasitaemia

| | Number (%) of children | | |
	With anaemia	With parasitaemia	Total
Net ownership			
no net	103 (54%)	132 (70%)	189
untreated net	90 (39%)	115 (49%)	233
treated net	70 (21%)	120 (37%)	326
Total	263	367	

Source: data from Abdulla *et al.* (2001)

Hint: Construct a 2 × 2 table of each outcome and exposure variable, and convert the exposure into two categories (i.e. net, no net; treated net, no treated net), as indicated in each question.

↻ Feedback

1 This is an analytical cross-sectional study, because the investigators are interested in the effect that the preventive measure of using insecticide-treated bed nets will have on the prevalence of malaria in children.

2 Yes, it might matter if data from children who could not be contacted or who refused to participate differed in some way from the data from children who were included. In fact, the investigators checked whether there were differences between those included in the analysis and those who were not by comparing net ownership and the prevalence of anaemia between these two groups, where they had data available, and found similar proportions in each group. However, they would be unable to check whether those who could not be contacted were similar to those who were interviewed, so there might be some bias in the results they reported. This would mean that their study population might differ from the target population (i.e. the general population to which the results are applied).

3 The results in Table 4.1 seem to indicate that ownership of treated nets increases over the period of the study, while the number of households with no nets or untreated nets decreases. The proportions of children with anaemia, parasitaemia and splenomegaly decrease over the course of the study. However, from Table 4.1 it is not possible to calculate the effect of net ownership on the proportion of children with malaria, because we have not been given the numbers of children with either anaemia, parasitaemia or splenomegaly in each of the net ownership categories.

4 Your 2 × 2 table should look like Table 4.3. To calculate the prevalence ratio, we need to compare the prevalence of anaemia in the two exposure groups:

Prevalence of anaemia in those with treated nets = 70/326 = 0.215 or 21.5%.

Prevalence of anaemia in those without treated nets = 193/422 = 0.457 or 45.7%.

Therefore the prevalence ratio is 0.215/0.457 = 0.47, indicating that children in households with treated nets have a 53% lower prevalence of anaemia than those without treated nets.

Table 4.3 Treated net ownership among children with and without anaemia

	Number of children		
	Anaemia	No anaemia	Total
Treated net	70	256	326
No treated net	193	229	422
Total	263	485	748

5 Your 2 × 2 table should look like Table 4.4.

Table 4.4 Net ownership among children with and without parasitaemia

	Number of children		
	Parasitaemia	No parasitaemia	Total
No net	132	57	189
Net	235	324	559
Total	367	381	748

To calculate the prevalence ratio, we need to compare the prevalence of parasitaemia in the two exposure groups:

Prevalence of parasitaemia in those without nets = 132/189 = 0.698 or 69.8%.

Prevalence of parasitaemia in those with nets = 235/559 = 0.420 or 42%.

Therefore the prevalence ratio is 0.698/0.420 = 1.66, indicating that children in households without nets have a 66% higher prevalence of parasitaemia than those with nets.

Summary

In this chapter you have learned about the key features of cross-sectional studies. You should now be able to describe the features of a cross-sectional study, discuss the potential sources of bias in this type of study, and understand its strengths and limitations.

In the next chapter, we will look at ecological studies.

Reference

Abdulla S, Armstrong Schellenberg J, Nathan R *et al.* (2001) Impact on malaria morbidity of a programme supplying insecticide treated nets in children aged under 2 years in Tanzania: community cross sectional study. *British Medical Journal* 322: 270–3.

5

Ecological studies

Overview

In this chapter you will learn about the features, advantages and limitations of ecological studies. Ecological studies are observational studies that can be descriptive or analytical and consider the characteristics of a disease and risk factors measured at the population rather than the individual level.

Learning objectives

After working through this chapter, you will be better able to:

- **describe the basic features and uses of ecological studies**
- **discuss the potential sources of bias in ecological studies**
- **understand the strengths and limitations of ecological studies.**

Key terms

Aetiology The science or philosophy of causation.

What is an ecological study?

The main difference between ecological studies and the other types of study we will look at is that they are carried out at the population level. They use aggregate data and do not measure outcomes and risk factors in individual people. Most ecological studies are cross-sectional in nature, and are used to compare different groups, such as populations from different regions or countries, or groups from different types of employment. These studies are known as *multigroup* studies. Some ecological studies are *longitudinal* in nature, which means that data are collected from a population over time to look for trends or changes. This type of study is known as a *time-trend* or a *time-series* study.

Like cross-sectional studies, ecological studies can be descriptive or analytical. A descriptive study might be used to look at the distribution of a particular outcome, such as cardiovascular disease or tuberculosis, across a geographic area for a multigroup study or in a particular region over time for a time-trend study, or between different subpopulations. The information from such studies can then be used to generate further research questions and hypotheses. Figure 5.1 shows how prevalence data can be used to show differences between geographic regions.

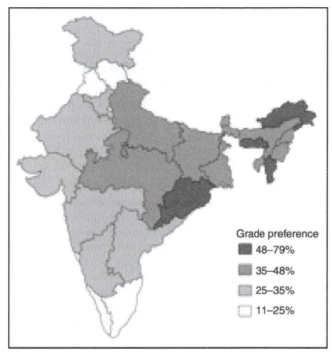

Figure 5.1 Distribution of tobacco consumption in India

Source: Subramanian *et al.* (2004)

Analytical ecological studies are used to investigate possible associations between exposures and outcomes at the population level. Again, this might be over time, as in a *time-trend study*, or between populations, as in a multigroup or geographical study.

Why study groups?

There are four main reasons why we might want to carry out an ecological between-group study:

- To investigate differences between populations: there may be greater differences between populations than within them – due to differences in culture or treatment, for example.
- To study group-specific effects: sometimes, especially in public health, interventions are aimed at the group level rather than the individual level.
- Convenience and availability of group-level data: sometimes data are only available at the group level (e.g. air pollution, health care services).
- It can be cheap and quick, especially if it uses routine data already available.

Multigroup study

In public health, in particular, we are often interested in explaining why some groups of people have a higher prevalence of disease than others. We can compare potential risk factors for disease between the groups to see whether they help to explain those differences.

Group-specific effects are exposures that act over the entire group, and do not necessarily have a direct effect on the individual members of the group. Ecological studies allow us to take account of exposures that act in this way. Examples of group-specific exposures include factors such as temperature and climate variation between regions, the presence of a public health measure or law, pollution, poverty, and even the regional prevalence of infectious diseases.

Routine data are often more easily obtainable at the group level than at the individual level. In addition, such data may be readily available, less costly and easier to use than individual data. Data on some exposures, such as those mentioned above, may be difficult or even impossible to collect at an individual level. They may also be more inaccurate than group-level data. For example, data on alcohol consumption for a population may be more accurately obtained by looking at alcohol sales across a region, rather than by asking individuals how much alcohol they drink (although there is no way of knowing whether the alcohol was consumed in the same time period).

Time-trend study

Comparisons can be made over time within the same population to show how incidence of disease changes over time and to identify patterns of change. Time-trend studies can investigate whether changes in disease incidence correlate with changes in risk factors for a disease or to evaluate a specific intervention. For example, does the increase or fluctuation in air quality correlate with the incidence of asthma in children?

Analysis and interpretation

In analytical ecological studies, measures of exposure and outcome are usually continuous variables: for example, prevalence of disease, mortality rate, proportion of population exposed to a particular factor, or mean temperature in a geographical region. This means that we cannot use the same measures as we would use in an individual-level study, such as a measure of relative risk. However, we can display the data as a scatterplot (see Figure 5.2) by plotting the outcome variable against the exposure variable. From this we can determine whether there seem to be any trends in the data, which can be confirmed using statistical methods (correlation or regression). Ecological studies can help us to draw conclusions about particular exposures on populations or groups of people. However, the results of ecological studies need to be interpreted with caution.

- Ecological studies may be unable to measure information on other important risk factors that may also be associated with the disease under study (because the data are collected already and were collected for other purposes). If this risk factor is also related to the risk factor under study it may confound the association between risk factor and disease and bias the result (confounding is explained in Chapter 9). Geographical comparisons can be standardized (direct or indirect standardization – see Chapter 2) for age and sex, but national estimates of prevalence may differ in other ways that are harder to measure (e.g. definitions of data collected).

• Data on exposure and outcome may be collected in different ways with different definitions which may bias the results. Differences in the way data are collected over time may also differ systematically. For example, definitions of a case or the diagnostic test used to identify a case may differ over time.

• Geographical comparisons may suffer from migration of populations between groups over the period of the study, which may dilute the difference between groups.

• Ecological studies do not enable us to answer questions about individual risks. Therefore, we should not assume that the causes of group-level outcomes are the same as the causes of individual cases. Any attempt to infer from the group level to the individual level – ecological inference – gives rise to *ecological fallacy* (or bias). For example, ecological studies have been used to show a relationship between breast cancer and higher proportion of fat in the diet, and we can say that these two are correlated, but we cannot say they are causally related and we cannot say that having a high fat intake causes breast cancer.

• Ecological studies are often criticized because of the problem of ecological fallacy. However, the same problem exists if we try to draw conclusions about group-level causes on the basis of results of an individual-level study. This is particularly important to remember when trying to change public health policy on the basis of individual-level data.

In the following activity, you will look at a study carried out in the late 1970s to look at a possible association between alcohol consumption and breast cancer in women.

✏ Activity 5.1

To assess the association between alcohol consumption and breast cancer, an epidemiological study involving 32 countries was carried out in 1978 (Schatzkin *et al.* 1989). The key methods of the study were as follows:

• to estimate the average per capita consumption of alcohol and fat during 1977 in several countries using the Food Balance Sheet of the Food and Agricultural Organization;

• to estimate the incidence of breast cancer in these populations in 1978 from the national cancer registries;

• to assess the association between the level of alcohol consumption and the incidence of breast cancer by linear regression methods.

The scatterplot in Figure 5.2 shows the incidence of breast cancer and alcohol consumption.

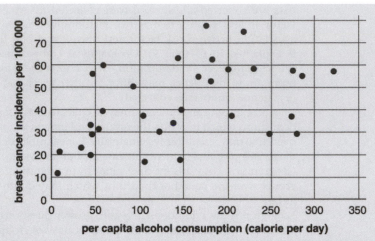

Figure 5.2 Correlation between alcohol consumption and incidence of breast cancer in 32 countries, 1978

Source: Schatzkin *et al.* (1989)

Table 5.1 gives the correlation coefficients obtained from the analysis. Correlation coefficients have values between −1 and +1: the further the value is from zero, the stronger the correlation, or association, between variables; therefore, a value above 0.6 (or below −0.6) indicates a strong positive (or negative) correlation, and a value between 0.4 and 0.6 indicates a moderate correlation.

Table 5.1 Correlation coefficients for alcohol and fat consumption and breast cancer, 1978

Variable	Correlation coefficient (r)	P-value
Breast cancer on alcohol	0.45	0.0091
Breast cancer on fat	0.69	0.0001
Breast cancer on alcohol adjusted for fat	−0.17	0.347

Source: Schatzkin *et al.* (1989)

Use the information given to answer the following questions:

1 What type of study is this? (Give reasons for your answer.)

2 Do the data in Table 5.1 suggest that there is an association between alcohol consumption and breast cancer?

3 Can you establish a causal link between alcohol consumption and breast cancer from this study? (Give reasons for your answer.)

 Feedback

Your answers should be along the following lines.

1 This is an *analytical* ecological study. It is an ecological study since the exposure variable of interest (alcohol) and the outcome variable (breast cancer) are measured

at the population level and the unit of analysis is populations (32 countries) and not individuals. And it is analytical because the study aims to assess the *association* (correlation) between the population level of alcohol consumption and the population incidence of breast cancer by linear regression methods.

2 The results of the correlation between breast cancer and alcohol consumption suggest that there is an association between these two variables. The likelihood of observing this association by chance is only 9 in 1000 (given by the *P*-value), so this association is statistically significant. However, when the correlation between fat consumption and breast cancer is taken into account, the correlation between alcohol and breast cancer is significantly reduced – indeed, the association is reversed (*r* = −0.17) and is not statistically significant (*P* = 0.347). It appears that the association between alcohol consumption and breast cancer was confounded by fat consumption.

3 No, it is not possible to establish such a causal link. Since the exposure variable (alcohol consumption) is not measured on individuals, the people who consumed alcohol and who developed breast cancer could be different within each population. Thus, a causal link cannot be established in this study design even if confounding is controlled by adjusting for other factors.

Summary

In this chapter you have learned about the key features of ecological studies. You should now be able to recognize an ecological study, and understand its strengths and limitations.

In the next chapter, we will look at cohort studies.

References

Schatzkin A, Piantadosi S, Miccozzi M, Bartee D (1989) Alcohol consumption and breast cancer: a cross-national correlation study. *International Journal of Epidemiology* 18(1): 28–31.

Subramanian SV, Nandy S, Kelly M, Gordon D, Davey Smith G (2004) Patterns and distribution of tobacco consumption in India: cross sectional multilevel evidence from the 1998–9 national family health survey. *British Medical Journal* 328: 801–6.

6

Cohort studies

Overview

One method of establishing an association between exposure and disease is to follow a population over time. In a cohort study, participants are followed over time to see whether they develop the disease of interest. Cohort studies have long been used as forms of natural experiment, since defined groups are followed as they would be in an intervention trial, although the investigator's job is purely to observe and not to intervene.

Learning objectives

After working through this chapter, you will be better able to:

- **describe the principal design features of cohort studies**
- **explain their strengths and weaknesses**
- **describe the major sources of bias of cohort studies**
- **describe the basic analytical approaches commonly used.**

Key terms

Measurement bias Systematic error in measurement or classification of the participants in a study.

Selection bias Systematic differences in characteristics of the participants in a study, between the study and control groups, so that they differ from each other by one or more factors that may affect the outcome of the study.

What is a cohort?

Epidemiologists use the term *cohort* to describe a group of individuals who share a common characteristic. A cohort may therefore be a group of workers from a factory, a group of children who were born in the same year, or a group of individuals who have been diagnosed with the same disease.

The cohort participants are selected on the basis of being exposed to a potential risk factor (e.g. work in the factory or not), and they should be free of the outcome under investigation at the start of the study. For example, if the outcome is having cancer, it is important to ensure that all participants are cancer-free at the start of the study.

In a cohort study, information on certain specified factors is collected at the start of the study and can be updated during the study. The progress of these individuals is then followed over time to see if they develop a particular disease or reach some other pre-specified end-point.

The cohort is defined by its exposure to a possible risk factor for the outcome under study. The exposure could be working in a particular factory, living in a city, or lifestyle factors such as smoking or alcohol intake. The outcome of interest could be developing a disease, or death, or possibly survival if the cohort all have a particular disease and the exposure of interest is some form of therapy.

Types of cohort study

Cohort studies (also known as *incidence studies, longitudinal studies, or follow-up studies*) are observational studies and can be descriptive or analytical. Cohort studies can be prospective or retrospective; however, both types define the cohort on the basis of exposure and not outcome status.

Prospective cohorts identify the participants and then follow them up over time until the end-point of interest has been reached (or the time limit for the study has been reached). This gives cohort studies an advantage over cross-sectional studies, because the temporal relationship between exposure and outcome can be established.

Retrospective cohorts use pre-existing data on exposures and outcomes – for example, from medical or occupational records – and therefore do not need to follow individuals over time since all the information is already available. A cohort study may combine both retrospective or prospective data. For example, an occupational cohort study may identify participants who started work in the same year and follow them until they retire, but may use data on previous work history and from medical records that pre-date the start of the study to provide information on exposures.

As with other studies (such as cross-sectional and ecological studies already discussed) there are advantages and disadvantages to using routine data. Retrospective studies using routine data are usually quicker and cheaper to carry out, particularly for diseases or events that may take decades to develop (e.g. cancer). Routine data may not be able to provide all the necessary information on other important risk factors for the disease under investigation (case mix), which, if unaccounted for, may lead to a bias in the study – for example, if the 'exposed' cohort are more likely to have this other risk factor than the 'unexposed' cohort. Routine data may have been poorly collected, with missing and inaccurate data. Data recorded over a long period of time may also be liable to changes in definitions and coding systems.

Study design

Selection of the study population

Selection of the study population usually depends on whether the exposure of interest is common or rare.

If the exposure is common, we can select the study population before classifying each individual as exposed or unexposed. The study population could be a sample of the general population, for example. Information on exposure can then be collected as the individuals are followed up, and the original selection of the cohort purely depends on the group being disease-free at the start of the study.

Alternatively, the study population could be selected from a particular occupation group (e.g. nurses, government workers, or mine workers) or by place of work (factory, or other large institution). This is known as a *workforce* or *occupational cohort* and has the advantage of higher participation and higher level of follow-up than general population cohorts. In most cases it does not matter that the work-force cohort is not representative of the general population, as long as the exposed and unexposed groups are comparable.

If the exposure is rare, the study sample can be selected on the basis of exposure to make sure that enough exposed people are included to make the study viable. For this type of study, occupational cohorts are usually very useful, especially if the exposure is connected to that type of occupation. For example, if the exposure of interest is contact with industrial chemicals, then workers at a particular factory who are known to handle chemicals as part of their job can be chosen as the exposure group. The comparison group would then be selected from workers at the same factory who did not work with those chemicals. This is known as an *internal comparison group*. However, if all workers at the factory had some degree of exposure, we would need to select a comparison group from another population, possibly another type of factory, to ensure that the comparison group only differed in terms of their exposure and not in terms of other factors. This would be an *external comparison group*.

The reason why we would tend to select an external comparison group from another workforce and not from the general population is because of the *healthy worker effect*. The general population is usually less healthy than a workforce population, because it includes people who are too sick to be at work. This will introduce additional differences between the two comparison groups, and may lead to bias in the results that are obtained. This type of bias is a form of *selection bias*. The effect of this phenomenon is that any excess risk associated with an occupation will tend to be underestimated by a comparison with the general population.

Exposures

As in any study, it is important that exposures are measured accurately and consistently between study participants. Failure to do so may result in another type of bias – *measurement (information) bias*.

Data on exposures can be collected in much same way as in a cross-sectional study – for example, by interviewing the participants, consulting medical records, taking biological samples, or using other forms of routine data. Usually data that are not going to change during the study are collected at the beginning, such as date of birth, sex, birth weight, adult height, blood type and genetic factors. Other data that may change, such as blood pressure, physical activity, smoking, or disease status, are collected by reassessing the cohort at predefined timepoints during the study, or in certain circumstances from medical records as and when they occur.

It may well be the case that the exposure of interest changes during the study. It is therefore important that any changes in exposure status are documented and updated. There are special statistical techniques that can be used in the analysis of results that will take account of such changes, and can even deal with changes in continuous variables such as blood pressure variations.

A major consideration when designing a cohort study is the availability of accurate and complete information that will allow the correct classification of exposure status and outcome status. The main feature of prospective cohort studies is that data on exposures are collected *before* data on the outcome. This gives them a major advantage over other study types in determining whether an exposure might be causally associated with the outcome, since we can be fairly sure in which order the exposure and outcome occurred and it is unlikely that the outcome status would affect the classification of exposure status. However, in retrospective cohort studies this may not be the case if knowledge of the disease status affects classification of exposure status. In addition, if the exposure status is known by the person assessing outcome status, this could lead to misclassification of outcome status (*observer bias*). More information about the effect of misclassification can be found in Chapter 9.

Follow-up

The length of follow-up that is needed for some studies to reach a satisfactory end-point, when a large enough proportion of the participants have reached an outcome, may be many years or even decades. This can make this type of study particularly expensive and time-consuming to carry out. That is why cohort studies often make use of occupational cohorts, for example, as keeping track of these individuals is easier, and the cost of following them up is often lower, than for a general population cohort. Retrospective studies can avoid some of the problems of a long follow-up period by using historical records. However, these data may be less accurate.

The length of time a cohort needs to be followed up leads to a potential weakness of cohort studies, because loss of contact with participants in the study can result in bias if there are differences in this *loss to follow-up* between exposure groups. This may be due to the people who are lost to follow-up being more (or less) likely to have developed the outcome of interest. If follow-up of participants is conducted by a self-completed questionnaire, for example, patients may be less likely to respond due to death, disability, moving into a nursing home, etc.

Outcomes

Again, as with other sorts of study, information on outcomes should be as complete and as accurate as possible for all exposure groups. These data should be collected without knowledge of exposure status, to avoid bias by those collecting the data (*observer bias*). Data collection methods for outcome may range from death notifications from routine databases, periodic health examinations or health outcome questionnaires to members of the cohort. The type of outcome collected needs to be appropriate to the disease under study.

Analysis

If the cohort study is descriptive, we can simply measure the frequency with which the outcome occurs. This could be either a *risk* or a *rate*. If the follow-up times for all the participants are similar, then we can use the risk. However, if the follow-up times differ between participants, then a rate would be more appropriate. (A rate uses person-time at risk so is more accurate if the person-time at risk differs across participants.)

In an analytical cohort study, the method of analysis depends on whether the exposure measures are categorical or continuous (see Chapter 4). Again, depending on the follow-up, we can then calculate a *risk ratio* or *rate ratio* (in the case of dichotomous variables) or even a measure of *attributable risk* or rate. Comparison of disease or death rates in the cohort with the rates in general population could also be made by using standardized morbidity or mortality ratios.

If the exposure measure has more than two levels or is continuous, we would need to decide which level to use as a baseline to compare against other levels. For example, non-smokers could be used as the baseline unexposed group, and levels of outcome compared against ex-smokers and current smokers.

As with any analytical study in epidemiology, the observed association between exposure and outcome may be affected by *chance, bias and confounding* and consideration needs to be given to how they may have affected the results.

There is a possibility that results witnessed are due to *chance* alone. Chance is more likely to be a factor if the sample size is small and the study lacks the *power* to detect the true estimation of the association (see Chapter 4 for more information on power and sample size). The role of chance in any study can be measured by a *P*-value given by a statistical test (e.g. a chi-square or *t* test) which represents the probability that an association (at least as big as the one observed) could have occurred by chance alone, given there truly was no association (null hypothesis).

The extent to which the observed association has been affected by bias needs to be evaluated – for example, if there were (systematic) differences in the way participants were selected (selection bias) or differences in the way exposure and outcome information was measured (measurement bias). Essentially, if the exposed and non-exposed groups differed in more ways than just their exposure status this will bias the true association between exposure and outcome. Inaccuracies in data collection and classification of exposure and outcome data are inevitable in any study; however, this biases the results when the errors are different for each study group.

Confounding may result in the strength of an association being over- or under-estimated. A *confounder* is a characteristic that is an independent risk factor for the outcome (disease) under study as well as being associated with the exposure under study. If one study group has a greater proportion of the confounder than the comparison group then that group will be more likely to develop the outcome under study even regardless of the true association between the exposure and outcome under study. If details of confounders are available for the participants then it is possible to take these into account during the analysis of the study. However, some confounders may not be known to the investigator or data may not be available on them (this is particularly a problem for retrospective cohort studies relying on routine data).

Further issues of interpretation will be discussed in Chapter 9.

Strengths and weaknesses

Cohort studies have the advantage that they can be used to study relatively rare exposures by careful selection of groups of participants on the basis of their exposure. This group can then be compared with another cohort that was unexposed to this risk factor to see whether they differ in terms of the incidence of disease.

Cohort studies also have flexibility in that they enable the investigators to study a wide range of disease outcomes that might be associated with the exposure of interest. Since they do not rely on data that have already been documented, the investigators can decide to collect a broad range of information, as long as they have the funds to do so. Another advantage is that if an outcome was not anticipated at the start of the study, this need not stop collection of data about it later on. In addition to information on outcomes, detailed information on confounding factors can be collected, allowing the investigators to control for them either in the design or analysis. If the data on exposures are very detailed, there may also be the opportunity to study dose–response relationships between exposures and outcomes.

Because of the way in which the study is carried out, information on exposure relates to time period before disease onset. Cohort studies are therefore more likely than ecological, cross-sectional or case–control studies to meet the temporality criterion for causality (see Chapter 9).

One major disadvantage of cohort studies is the number of participants (sample size) that is required. If the disease is rare, the sample size may have to be so large that a cohort study is impracticable, and other study designs may need to be considered, such as a case–control study.

Another disadvantage is the cost of data collection, although this depends on whether the study is retrospective, prospective or a mixture of the two, and on whether follow-up is active (e.g. health evaluations, quality-of-life questionnaires) or passive (e.g. death or cancer notifications).

The time required to carry out a cohort study may also be a disadvantage, since this is likely to be substantially longer than for other study designs. Some prospective cohort studies may take many decades to complete. However, investigators often try to work round this by trying to obtain the maximum benefits from such a study by collecting as much data as possible so that other substudies can be carried out using the same cohort.

Because of the strengths and weaknesses listed above, cohort studies are most often used when the disease of interest is common or the effects of the exposure are non-specific or not well defined.

✎ Activity 6.1

In 1951, a prospective cohort study was set up among British doctors to investigate the relationship between smoking and mortality, particularly the association between smoking and lung cancer (Doll and Peto 1976; Doll *et al.* 1980). This is an important study and follow-up of participants is still under way. Results for 50 years of follow-up were published recently in the *British Medical Journal* (Doll *et al.* 2004).

In 1951, a questionnaire on smoking habits was sent to 49,913 male and 10,323 female doctors registered with the British General Medical Council; 34,440 (69%) male doctors and 6194 female doctors gave sufficient information to classify their smoking status. The vital status of these doctors was followed up for 50 years from the records of the Registrar General's Office, the British Medical Council, and the British Medical Association. The causes of death of 10,072 male and 1094 female doctors who had died during this period were ascertained from death certificates. The rate of death from lung cancer among smokers was compared to that among non-smokers.

1 Discuss the potential sources of bias in this study.

2 What information on smoking would you collect to classify smoking exposure status?

3 The numbers of male doctors in each age group classified as smokers or non-smokers are given in Table 6.1. Comment on the age distribution and the steps to be taken while comparing lung cancer deaths between these two groups.

Table 6.1 Numbers of smokers and non-smokers by age group among the male doctors

Age group (years)	Smokers	Non-smokers	Total
20–29	3 568	1 693	5 261
30–39	8 057	1 884	9 941
40–49	6 310	1 030	7 340
50–59	5 144	610	5 754
60–69	3 082	288	3 370
70+	2 476	298	2 774
Total	28 637	5 803	34 440

Source: data based on Doll and Peto (1976)

4 Age-adjusted lung cancer death rates (per 100,000 persons per year) among smokers and non-smokers in male and female doctors are given in Table 6.2. Calculate an appropriate epidemiological measure to assess the association between smoking and lung cancer and discuss the result, especially the differences between males and females.

Table 6.2 Death rates from lung cancer by status of smoking and sex

| Sex of doctors | Lung cancer death rates per 100 000 persons per year* | | | |
	Non-smokers	Smoking 1–14 cigarettes/day	Smoking 15–24 cigarettes/day	Smoking 25+ cigarettes/day
Male	10	78	127	251
Female	7	9	45	208

* Adjusted for age by direct standardization.

Source: based on Doll and Peto (1976) and Doll et al. (1980)

5   The proportion of inhalers of smoke and the mean age when started to smoke among the three groups of smokers in men and women are given in Table 6.3. What further analysis would be needed to explore further the observed difference in the effect of moderate smoking in men and women?

Table 6.3 Distribution of inhalation and mean age when started to smoke

| Features of smoking | Smoking 1–14 cigarettes/day | | Smoking 15–24 cigarettes/day | | Smoking 25+ cigarettes/day | |
	Male	Female	Male	Female	Male	Female
Proportion inhaling smoke (%)	66	42	80	54	83	58
Mean age (years) when started to smoke	20	24	19	23	19	22

Source: based on Doll and Peto (1976) and Doll et al. (1980)

 Feedback

Your answers to the questions should be along the lines of the following:

1 There are two potential sources of bias in this study. Some doctors might have given inaccurate information regarding their smoking habits which could have resulted in misclassification of exposure to smoking (*information bias*). However, the size of this bias and its influence on the observed association between smoking and lung cancer would be small, since at the time of classification of exposure to smoking, the risk of lung cancer (the outcome) was not known. It is possible that lung cancer was more frequently diagnosed or certified as the cause of death among smokers than among non-smokers. However, this is unlikely since lung cancer can be diagnosed accurately using various radiographic and histological investigations.

It is unlikely that the investigators were able to follow up all subjects for 20 years for reasons such as migration and loss of records (*loss to follow-up*). In this study, however, the rate of loss to follow-up is unlikely to be different between smokers and non-smokers.

2 First, the subjects have to be classified as current, past or never smokers. In addition, the effect of smoking can vary depending on the type of smoke (e.g. cigarette, cigar),

quantity of smoke (number of cigarettes per day; duration of smoking; method of smoking, for example inhalation), age when started to smoke, and age when stopped (if stopped). Information on all these variables related to smoking has to be collected.

3 The proportions of doctors in the age groups 20–29 years and 30–39 years are substantially lower among smokers than non-smokers; in the other age groups, the proportions are higher among smokers than non-smokers (Table 6.4).

Table 6.4 Distribution of doctors by age group among smokers and non-smokers

Age group (years)	Smokers	Non-smokers	Total population
20–29	3 568 (12%)	1 693 (29%)	5 261 (15%)
30–39	8 057 (28%)	1 884 (32%)	9 941 (29%)
40–49	6 310 (22%)	1 030 (18%)	7 340 (21%)
50–59	5 144 (18%)	610 (11%)	5 754 (17%)
60–69	3 082 (11%)	288 (5%)	3 370 (10%)
70+	2 476 (9%)	298 (5%)	2 774 (8%)
Total	28 637	5 803	34 440

Source: based on Doll and Peto (1976) and Doll et al. (1980)

Since mortality depends on age and the distribution of subjects by age group is different between the smokers and non-smokers, the effect of age on mortality has to be adjusted for when making comparison on lung cancer mortality between these two groups. A commonly used method to adjust for the age is direct standardization (see Chapter 2).

4 An appropriate epidemiological measure to assess the association between smoking and lung cancer is relative risk – in this case, the rate ratio of lung cancer death among different levels of smokers in male and females using the rate of death in non-smokers as the baseline would be appropriate (Table 6.5).

Table 6.5 Relative risk of lung cancer death (adjusted for age) by status of smoking in male and female doctors

Sex	Non-smokers	Smoking 1–14 cigarettes/day	Smoking 15–24 cigarettes/day	Smoking 25+ cigarettes/day
Male	1	7.8	12.7	25.1
Female	1	1.3	6.4	29.7

Source: based on Doll and Peto (1976) and Doll et al. (1980)

The relative risk of lung cancer death increased with the level of smoking in both males and females. The relative risk in the men smoking 1–14 and 15–24 cigarettes per day is much higher than in the women; in the group smoking 25 or more cigarettes per day, the relative risk in men is marginally less than that in women. Does this mean that the effect of low levels of smoking is higher among men than among women? No statistical testing to rule out the role of chance has been carried out, but the study had a large sample size and the magnitude of difference is high, so it is unlikely to be due to chance. However, the estimation of level of exposure to tobacco by counting the number of cigarettes smoked per day may not be appropriate. For instance, the duration of smoking, inhalation practices and age when started to smoke might have been different between the men and women. Unless the effects of these features of smoking are taken into account, one cannot conclude that low to moderate smoking has a higher effect in men than in women.

5 The proportion of men inhaling smoke is higher than women in all three levels of smoking. Men seemed to have started to smoke at an earlier age than women. Since these features of smoking may modify the effect of smoking on lung cancer, their effects have to be adjusted for when comparing the association between smoking and lung cancer in men and women.

Summary

In this chapter, you have learned about the key features of cohort studies. You should now be able to describe the features of a cohort study, discuss the potential sources of bias in this type of study, and understand its strengths and limitations.

In the next chapter, we will look at case–control studies.

References

Doll R, Peto R (1976) Mortality in relation to smoking: 20 years' observation on male British doctors. *British Medical Journal* ii: 1525–36.

Doll R, Gray R, Hafner B, Peto R (1980) Mortality in relation to smoking: 22 years' observations on female British doctors. *British Medical Journal* 280: 967–71.

Doll R, Peto R, Boreham J, Sutherland I (2004) Mortality in relation to smoking: 50 years' observations on male British doctors. *British Medical Journal* 328: 1519–27.

7

Case–control studies

Overview

Another type of analytical observational epidemiological study is the case–control study. Case–control studies, first developed in the early 1950s, avoid some of the disadvantages of cohort studies, particularly the length of time that they take to complete and, in the case of a rare disease, the need for a large study population.

Learning objectives

After working through this chapter, you will be better able to:

- **describe the principal design features of case–control studies**
- **explain their strengths and weaknesses**
- **recognize the importance of clearly defining cases and controls**
- **describe the major sources of bias of case–control studies**
- **describe the basic analytical approaches commonly used.**

Key terms

Cases Individuals in a population who have the outcome of interest (e.g. disease, health disorder, or event such as heart attack or death). Case definition should include clearly defined inclusion and exclusion criteria.

Controls (in a case-control study) Individuals who do not have the outcome of interest, and used as the comparison group in analytical studies.

Study design

In case–control studies, the study group is defined by the outcome and not by exposure. Two or more groups are selected on the basis of whether they do (cases) or do not (controls) have the disease or other outcome under study at the *beginning* of the study. The cases are then compared with controls to assess whether they are different in terms of their historical exposure to particular risk factors.

One of the advantages of case–control studies is that they can be used to study diseases or outcomes that are rare. Since participants are selected on their disease status, the minimum number of cases and controls required can be established before the study begins. A cohort study would require the follow-up of prohibitively large numbers of individuals to ensure that enough participants develop the outcome. Another advantage is that case–control studies can be more efficient than cohort studies when there is a long period of time between the exposure and disease (latency period), as in chronic diseases (e.g. cancer). This is because information on the exposure and outcome status is already present at the start of the study and does not entail a long period of follow-up. Case–control studies can also investigate the association between the disease and multiple exposures as the patients are identified with the disease and then followed back in time for details of previous exposures. Improvements in techniques mean that case–control studies are also being used to study infectious diseases and injuries.

One of the problems with case–control studies is that both the exposure and the disease have occurred by the time the patient is recruited into the study (participants are selected on the basis of their disease status). This makes case–control studies susceptible to selection bias (if cases and controls are selected differentially on the basis of their exposure status and because there may be differences in reporting of exposure status between cases and controls).

Hypothesis

The definition of the hypothesis, or research question to be answered, is probably more important in this type of study than in any other, since the selection of study participants depends so closely on the question that the investigators want to answer. As participants are selected on the basis of their outcome and will be compared by their exposure, it is important that the participants represent the exposure prevalence of the general population and that the study is not biased by the selection of cases and controls being influenced by their exposure (selection bias).

Selection of cases

Case definition

It is important in case–control studies to obtain a precise definition of a *case*. The criteria used might be based on laboratory data, for example, biopsy samples, or might depend on clinical diagnosis of the disease. Such inclusion and exclusion criteria must be clearly stated before the study is carried out to ensure that the practice of identifying cases is kept uniform throughout the study.

Prevalent and incident cases

One important issue to consider when designing a study is whether both incident and prevalent cases should be included. Inclusion of prevalent cases may mean that the study is more *generalizable* to the standard population, as the prevalent cases reflect a proportion of cases in the population. However, prevalent cases may differ from incident cases in ways that may reduce the *validity* of the study.

Inclusion of prevalent cases, especially people who have had the disease for a long period of time, may pose problems in terms of determining their exposure to certain risk factors, since it is possible that they may have changed their exposure habits as a result of the disease (e.g. their diet or exercise regime). Investigators should take precautions to make sure that unbiased data on exposures are collected (observer bias).

Inclusion of prevalent cases may also lead to an underrepresentation of more severe cases of the disease. This is because patients with rapidly progressive disease may die very soon after diagnosis and be less likely to be selected for the study. This in turn may affect the exposures that are under study, since any risk factors associated with longer survival will also become linked with the disease outcome, even if they might be protective against the development of severe disease.

Source

Another important consideration is the source of cases. If a disease is particularly severe, it may mean that cases are only found in hospitals. Alternatively, cases may be selected from the general population through disease notification processes – for instance, public health records of food poisoning or notifiable diseases such as hepatitis – or through family practitioners' records. Population-based studies are often easier to interpret because controls can be selected from the same population, with less danger of selecting on possible exposure status. However, they can be more difficult to carry out than a hospital-based study.

Ultimately, it is important to ensure that the cases selected for a study are truly representative of all cases in the population under study. Failure to do so may result in selection bias. The following factors may cause selection bias in the selection of cases:

- patient survival – if the disease is fatal, it is important to ensure that patients who have died are included
- referrals to specialist hospitals – if the disease is rare or unusual, it is important to make sure that all locations of patients are identified
- refusals – patients who refuse to take part in the study may differ in some crucial way from those who agree to take part in the study.

Selection of controls

Inclusion criteria

Selection of suitable controls is probably the most difficult part of designing a case–control study. Controls should meet all the criteria for cases, except for the disease itself. For example, if the cases are men aged 40–65 years with lung cancer, the controls must be selected from men of that age group who do not have lung cancer.

Source

The source of controls depends on the source of cases. If the cases were selected from the general population, then the controls should be randomly selected from this population during the same time period. However, it is less clear what to do if the cases were selected from a hospital setting, and this will depend on the disease or condition that is under study. If all people who contract a particular disease end up in hospital, and there is no other selection process involved in the cases reaching hospital other than the disease and the exposures under consideration, then controls can be selected from the general population.

If there is a selection process involved, then it may be more appropriate to recruit controls from among other hospital patients, as long as their selection is not then biased in terms of the exposure of interest. For example, we may want to investigate risk factors for liver cirrhosis. If we suspect heavy alcohol use to be a major risk factor and select cases from hospital records, we may have problems if our hospital-based controls include a large proportion of people admitted to hospital for trauma, since people admitted for this reason are known to be more likely to be heavy users of alcohol than the general population.

Matching

One way to select suitable controls is to match a small group (usually four or fewer people) to each case on the basis of certain factors that might be related to the disease and the exposure. This is known as *individual matching*. Factors such as age and sex are usually chosen, and other factors such social status, or place of residence (as a proxy for socioeconomic status) may also be used, depending on the aim of the study. However, it is important not to select too many characteristics on which to match, or to select factors that might be very closely associated with exposure status, since any factors that are used for matching cannot then be included in the analysis. Matching may also make the study more time-consuming and more expensive to carry out.

An alternative to individual matching is *group matching* (or frequency matching), in which the control group is selected so that it is similar to the cases with respect to the matched variable. For example, if we group-matched by sex and our cases were 60% female, we would ensure that the controls were also 60% female. However, in a matched study, we have to be careful to avoid *overmatching*. This occurs when the matching variable is closely related to the exposure variable, but is not related to the outcome.

Cohort studies

Cases that arise during a cohort study can be used as the basis for a *nested case–control study*. In this design, unaffected members of the cohort are used as controls, and are thereby automatically matched on factors common to all cohort members. For instance, in an occupational cohort study, cases and controls will be matched on employment status simply by virtue of being in that cohort. This form of study design also means that new hypotheses can be tested more easily, since data on exposures is likely to have already been collected, which in turn will also save time and money.

Measuring exposures

Since case–control studies start with assessment of the outcome, collection of information on exposures is almost always retrospective. In this way, case–control studies are often very like cross-sectional studies in the way in which data are collected, especially since data on outcomes and exposure are often collected simultaneously.

Exposure data can be gathered in many different ways, including by interview (face-to-face, telephone, postal, or even e-mail), from records (medical, work, or other sources), or by taking biological samples. Ideally, someone who does not know whether the study participant is a case or control should collect information on exposure, although in practice this is difficult to achieve. In any case, the procedure by which information is collected should be identical for cases and controls to avoid bias (in this case, observer bias).

Another form of bias common when obtaining information about exposures is *reporting bias* (this is sometimes referred to as *responder bias*; take care not to confuse this with response/non-response bias, which is the failure of participants to respond to questionnaires and is a form of selection bias). Reporting bias occurs when knowledge of being a case (or control) affects whether the individual remembers a certain event or exposure (also known as *recall bias*). For example, cases may be more likely to remember events that occurred at around the time they were diagnosed with disease or underwent a traumatic event. Controls may therefore be less likely to remember an event because by definition they have no disease event to link it to.

Temporal bias (also known as *reverse causality*) may also be involved in the collection of exposure data. In establishing any causal link between exposure and outcome, the investigator must be sure that any risk factor occurred well before an individual was diagnosed with disease. Because case–control studies often rely on the retrospective collection of data once cases have been identified, there is a chance that the disease caused the exposure to occur before symptoms of disease were identified. This may also be a problem with infectious diseases with a long incubation period (e.g. HIV). This was also mentioned above in relation to the inclusion of prevalent disease amongst cases.

A nested case–control design may help to overcome most of the biases outlined above. The main advantage of this sort of study is that information on exposures is likely to have been collected at the start of the study (at baseline), before cases had been diagnosed. This means that it is easier to establish a causal link between exposure and outcome. It also means that recall and observer bias are less likely to occur.

Analysis and interpretation

Data analysis

Unlike cohort studies, case–control studies cannot directly estimate the incidence of disease in exposed and unexposed individuals, because study participants are selected on the basis of their disease status and not on the basis of their exposure.

This means that the outcome measure of a case–control study is the *odds ratio of exposure* (see Chapter 3), which is the odds of exposure in the cases divided by the odds of exposure in the controls. If the disease is rare and the exposure reasonably common, this measure is approximately equal to the risk ratio.

If the study is matched, then a more complicated analysis needs to be performed that takes account of the matching. In this type of analysis, only the matched groups that provide useful information (i.e. a case–control pair where either the case is exposed and the control unexposed, or the case is unexposed and the control exposed) are compared to give an odds ratio of exposure.

Interpretation

Even if an association between exposure and outcome is found, the investigator still has to consider whether the result could have arisen by chance, or whether it was the result of bias or confounding.

Bias

As we have seen above, case–control studies are particularly prone to bias, and this should always be considered as an explanation for the findings of a study. Investigators therefore need to take care to ensure that cases and controls are comparable, and to limit the effects of selection bias, information bias (observer and reporting bias) and temporal bias.

Confounding

A confounder is a factor that is associated with both the exposure and the outcome, but is not on the causal pathway between them. You learned a little about confounding in Chapter 2 when you calculated standardized mortality ratios. Confounding is a problem when cases and controls differ with respect to the potential confounding variable. This can either be dealt with at the design stage, by matching, or at the analysis stage, by adjusting the analysis for the confounders using statistical techniques.

Strengths and weaknesses

The main advantage of case–control studies is that they can be carried out more quickly and cheaply than cohort studies. Case–control studies are also useful for studying rare diseases. If the disease is rare and the exposure is common, the odds ratio provided will be a good approximation to the risk ratio. They can be used to study diseases with long latent periods, and can also be used to study multiple exposures.

However, case–control studies are prone to bias. Selection bias can occur particularly in the selection of controls, and information bias in the determination of exposures. They are also poor at establishing causal associations because data on exposure and outcome are usually recorded simultaneously. Because case–control studies start with the selection of cases, they are not suitable for studying rare exposures, unless they form part of a cohort study (nested case–control study). Case–control studies cannot be used to estimate disease incidence or prevalence.

 Activity 7.1

The activities in this chapter relate to a review of epidemiological studies of the association between alcohol consumption and breast cancer. The review identified 27 case–control studies, 8 cohort studies and 5 ecological studies that had been carried out on this issue between 1977 and 1992 (Rosenberg et al. 1993).

Why do you think more investigators preferred the case–control study design over the other designs?

 Feedback

Since the outcome variable (breast cancer) has a long latent period and is relatively uncommon, the case–control design is more appropriate than the cohort design, because the latter would need more resources and time. Furthermore, breast cancer is known to be associated with several risk factors and the case–control design allows you to investigate multiple risk factors. An ecological study may be used initially to generate the research question by indicating a possible link between breast cancer and alcohol, but it would not be able to establish a causal link.

 Activity 7.2

It is now well accepted that early age at menarche, late age at menopause, nulliparity (never having had a live or still birth), and late age at first birth are risk factors for breast cancer in women. Among the 27 case–control studies that have been carried out to investigate the possible association between breast cancer and alcohol consumption, some have found a statistically significant association between alcohol consumption and an increased risk of breast cancer in women, whereas others have found no association or have been inconclusive.

One of the studies included in the review investigated the relation between alcohol and breast cancer in women in northern Europe. Between January 1989 and December 1990, 161 women aged under 75 years were treated for newly diagnosed, histologically confirmed breast cancer at four hospitals in the area. Of these women, 29 could not be interviewed: 10 because the patient refused, 10 because their consultant refused, and 9 because the patient was too ill to be interviewed. The remaining 132 women were interviewed as inpatients within 6 months of diagnosis by one of six interviewers. At the start of the study, the investigators decided to recruit four times as many controls as cases, and selected as controls 528 women who were attending the same hospital for other conditions.

Data on socioeconomic characteristics, medical, reproductive and menstrual history, and other potential risk factors for breast cancer were collected using a structured questionnaire. The questionnaire also included detailed questions on smoking and drinking. The interviewers were aware of the hypothesis, and which women were cases and which were controls.

In this study, the controls were not individually matched to the cases, although the investigators decided to ensure that the age distribution of the controls was approximately the same as that of the cases by the end of the study. The data were analysed using an unmatched approach, by comparing the odds of exposure to alcohol consumption between cases and controls, and then adjusting for the effect of potential confounding factors.

1   Why do you think that cases in the study were restricted to:

a) women who had been diagnosed with breast cancer in the 6 months before the interview, and
b) women who were inpatients?

2   If you were designing the questionnaire for this study, what information on alcohol consumption would you ask for? Are there any other questions you would have considered it necessary to ask?

3   If you had been one of the investigators on the study, what source would you have used for your controls, and what would your inclusion and exclusion criteria have been?

4   Would you have matched the controls to cases, and if so, what would your matching variables have been?

5   How might the interviewers' awareness of the hypothesis and the identity of the cases and controls have biased the study? Explain how the study could have been designed to minimize this bias.

↻ Feedback

Your answers to the questions should be along the following lines:

1   a) Women were interviewed within 6 months of diagnosis, so that only incident cases of breast cancer were included in the study. As you will have read above, it is important to decide in the design of a study whether to include incident or prevalent cases. Inclusion of prevalent cases may lead to bias if those women have changed their behaviour and therefore their exposure to risk factors as a result of their disease, and this is picked up by the questionnaire. Restricting the study to incident cases also ensures that severe cases are not underrepresented.

   b) The important consideration here is whether the cases are representative of all cases in the general population. Although selection of population-based cases may result in a study that is less prone to bias, the logistics and costs involved may make it easier to identify cases in a hospital setting, particularly cases of a rare disease such as cancer. There is then the consideration of whether those with the disease under investigation are likely to be admitted to hospital. Women with breast cancer are almost certain to be referred or admitted to hospital once diagnosed, so selection of hospital-based cases is appropriate in this study.

2 In designing a questionnaire, you would need to consider what information is needed, and how you would ask the questions to overcome any potential problems that might lead to measurement and recall bias. It is well known, for example, that people tend to underreport their alcohol consumption.

You may consider collecting the following information related to alcohol consumption:

- whether the participant is a current, past, or never drinker
- what type of alcohol they consume (e.g. beer, wine, spirits)
- what quantity of alcohol they consume (e.g. number of drinks per day)
- how long an average drinking session might last (e.g. number of hours per day)
- how often they drink (e.g. number of days per week)
- what age they started drinking, and what age when they stopped drinking (if they stopped).

Note that you may need to convert alcohol consumption into standard units so that your results are comparable with other studies.

Other questions that you would need to ask are those that would give basic demographic information about the participants: for example, date of birth, education and occupation. You would also need to ask about possible confounders: for example, smoking and known risk factors for breast cancer (age at menarche, age at menopause, number of pregnancies, and age at first birth).

3 As noted in the text, selection of controls is a complicated issue. In general, investigators find it convenient to select controls in the same setting in which they selected the cases, and in this study the investigators have indeed selected controls from among hospital patients. However, it is important that the study is not then biased by selecting controls that are more similar to the cases in terms of their exposure than they would have been if selected from the general population. In a hospital setting, there is the risk that inclusion of trauma patients or those with chronic liver disease in the controls may increase the proportion of those with exposure to excessive alcohol use compared with the general population, since this may then lead to an underestimation of the effect of this exposure in cases. Some hospital-based studies use two control groups, one from a hospital setting and the other from the population. Then if the selection of controls within the hospital setting is carried out without bias, the results should not differ depending on which control group was used in the data analysis. However, if the results do differ between the control groups, interpretation can be a problem.

Any exclusion criteria that apply to cases should also apply to controls: for example, women aged over 74 years, and women with previous breast cancer. You may also consider excluding patients who are admitted to hospital with alcohol-related diseases, and diseases related to known risk factors for breast cancer (e.g. gynaecological diseases). Many case–control studies of a specific cancer also exclude controls with any sort of cancer. In hospital-based studies, it is important to include controls with a range of different diseases so that no one disease is unduly represented.

4 You might want to match on age. The investigators made sure that the cases and controls at least had a similar age distribution by checking that the average age was similar in both groups. You could also match on known risk factors for breast cancer (e.g. parity). However, this can be difficult, and there is the need to be careful not to overmatch (i.e. match on alcohol status by mistake).

5 The investigators' knowledge of the hypothesis might lead to observer bias. This is because the investigators may be more inclined to ask more probing questions about alcohol use if they are aware of whether the participant was a case. This type of bias can be minimized by:

- blinding the interviewers to the hypothesis
- blinding the interviewers to the identity of the cases and controls, although this is often very difficult
- using a small number of interviewers to prevent too much variation between observers
- using standard questionnaires if possible
- ensuring that the interviewers are rigorously trained.

 Activity 7.3

The distribution of potential confounding factors is given in Table 7.1.

Table 7.1 Distribution of potential confounding variables among cases and controls

Confounding variables	Number (%)	
	Cases	Controls
Age (years)		
<45	28 (21%)	109 (21%)
45–64	72 (54%)	274 (52%)
65+	32 (24%)	145 (27%)
Occupation		
professional	16 (12%)	42 (8%)
clerical/manual worker	50 (38%)	285 (54%)*
housewife	66 (50%)	201 (38%)*
Parity		
never had a delivery	19 (14%)	55 (10%)
had at least one delivery	113 (86%)	437 (90%)
Age at first birth (years)		
< 22	29 (26%)	162 (34%)*
22+	84 (74%)	311 (64%)*

* $P < 0.05$, indicating a significant difference between cases and controls.

Source: data from Rosenberg et al. (1993)

1 Comment on the distribution of these variables. Think about whether you might need to adjust for their effect on breast cancer while estimating the effect of alcohol consumption.

The odds of exposure to number of drinks per day among cases and controls observed in this study are given in Table 7.2.

2 Complete the table by calculating the odds ratios, using the 'none' category as the reference, and comment on the results. Suggest what further analysis you would do. (We suggest you complete your answers to this question before looking at the next question.)

Table 7.2 Odds of exposure to alcohol among cases and controls

Number of drinks per day	Cases	Controls	Odds ratio
None	17	81	1.00
1	30	134	
2	45	163	
3+	40	130	

Source: data from Rosenberg *et al.* (1993)

The unadjusted and adjusted odds ratios for alcohol consumption in cases compared with controls are given in Table 7.3. The unadjusted odds ratios are the crude odds ratios you calculated in Question 2. The adjusted odds ratio have been calculated by taking into account the differences in distribution of potential confounding variables between cases and controls (see Table 7.1).

3 Comment on these results.

Table 7.3 Odds ratios of alcohol consumption in cases compared to controls

			Unadjusted		Adjusted*	
Number of drinks per day	Cases	Controls	Odds ratio	95% confidence interval	Odds ratio	95% confidence interval
None	17	81	1.00		1.00	
1	30	134	1.07	0.53–2.17	1.00	0.50–2.31
2	45	163	1.32	0.68–2.56	1.20	0.60–2.73
3+	40	130	1.47	0.75–2.90	1.41	0.71–3.00

* Adjusted for the effects of age, occupation, parity, age at first birth.

Source: data from Rosenberg *et al.* (1993)

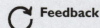

Feedback

Your answers to the questions should be along the following lines:

1 There is a statistically significant difference in the distribution of occupation and age at first birth between cases and controls. At the same time, although not statistically significant, the proportion of cases who have never had a delivery is higher among cases (14%) than among controls (10%). There is no significant difference in the distribution of age groups between cases and controls. Since all these factors are known to be associated with breast cancer, their effect on breast cancer should be controlled for when estimating the effect of alcohol consumption on breast cancer. It is reasonable to argue that the effect of age and parity need not be controlled since the distribution of these variables did not differ between cases and controls. However, since there are slight differences and this can lead to residual confounding, it is appropriate to control for their effect.

2 Your completed table should look like Table 7.4. The odds of exposure to alcohol seem to be higher among the cases than the controls. The odds ratio of alcohol consumption shows an increasing trend with increasing number of drinks per day. However, it is not appropriate to conclude that alcohol consumption is associated with breast cancer without considering the role of chance, bias and confounding (see Chapter 9 for more on chance, bias and confounding). The role of chance can be assessed by appropriate statistical tests. The effects of the potential confounding factors can be adjusted by stratified analysis.

Table 7.4 Odds of exposure to alcohol among cases and controls

Number of drinks per day	Cases	Controls	Odds ratio
None	17	81	1.00
1	30	134	1.07
2	45	163	1.32
3+	40	130	1.47

Source: data from Rosenberg et al. (1993)

3 The odds of alcohol consumption are slightly higher among the cases than the controls. However, this association is not statistically significant – the confidence intervals for the odds ratios range from less than 1 to greater than 1. Although the magnitude of odds ratios decreased when adjusted for the effect of the potential confounding factors, the increasing trend in odds ratios for increasing number of drinks persisted. However, the observed association between alcohol consumption and breast cancer is rather weak, and the role of chance and confounding by other factors (such as dietary habits and smoking) that were not controlled for cannot be excluded.

Summary

In this chapter you have learned about the key features of case–control studies. You should now be able to describe the features of a case–control study, understand the importance of the selection of cases and controls, discuss the potential sources of bias, and understand the strengths and limitations of this sort of study.

In the next chapter, you will look at intervention studies.

Reference

Rosenberg L, Metzger LS, Palmer JR (1993) Alcohol consumption and risk of breast cancer: a review of the epidemiologic evidence. *Epidemiologic Reviews* 15: 133–44.

8 Intervention studies

Overview

All the study types you have learned about so far have been passive and observational in nature. Intervention studies differ because they are designed to evaluate the effect of a specific therapy or public health practice in a well-defined population. In effect, they are epidemiological experiments.

Learning objectives

After working through this session, you will be better able to:

- describe the main design features and types of intervention studies
- decide when it would and would not be appropriate to use an intervention study
- explain the strengths and weaknesses of this study design
- understand the ways in which intervention studies can be designed to maximize their usefulness and validity
- describe the basic analytical approaches commonly used
- discuss the ethical issues concerning intervention studies.

Key terms

Randomization The process of allocating patients to treatment based on chance. It is not possible for the investigator, clinician or patient to predict the allocation in advance.

What is an intervention study?

Intervention studies are designed so that the effect of a specific therapy or public health practice can be evaluated in a well-defined population. In effect they are epidemiological experiments because, unlike the other sorts of studies we have looked at so far, the participants of the study are actively allocated treatments by the investigators. In all the other study types you have learned about in previous chapters the investigator generally has no influence on the type of treatment a patient is given, so is observational in this respect.

Intervention studies can be used to test new drugs or vaccines, to evaluate prevention strategies, and to test health education methods, training procedures or other public health programmes. Care needs to be taken in their design to ensure that any findings are unambiguous, and that results can be broadly applied in a chosen population.

Types of intervention study

There are two main types of intervention study, therapeutic studies and preventive studies. *Therapeutic studies* are designed to test the effect of therapies, which could be new drugs, surgery or vaccines, in people who already have a particular disease. These studies are also referred to as *clinical trials*. *Preventive studies* designed to evaluate prevention strategies, on the other hand, are carried out on people who do not necessarily have a particular disease but are considered 'at risk'. These studies are also referred to as *field trials*, and may take the form of a trial to test health education methods, training procedures or other public health programmes.

Studies to test new drugs or surgical procedures are conducted in four phases. Phase 1 studies introduce a new drug to humans (usually healthy volunteers) to determine how a drug should be administered (e.g. by mouth, injection into the blood, or injection into the muscle). They also review side effects, safety and the dosage of the drug, and are usually only carried out on a small numbers of people. Phase 2 studies continue to evaluate efficacy and safety in selected populations of about 100–300 patients who have the disease or condition to be treated, diagnosed, or prevented. Participants tend to be hospitalized patients who can be closely monitored. The focus is on dose–response relationships, type of patient, frequency of dosing, or any of a number of other issues involved in safety and efficacy. Phase 2a studies are pilot clinical trials and Phase 2b studies are well controlled trials. Phase 3 of a clinical trial is an intervention study to test a new drug, a new combination of drugs, or a new surgical procedure in comparison to the current standard. These are often large studies and participants are assigned to the treatment groups by randomization. Finally, phase 4 studies are post-marketing studies to delineate additional information including the drug's risks, benefits and optimal use.

Intervention studies can also be carried out on individuals or groups (clusters such as GP practices). In this chapter, we will mainly look at individual-level studies.

Study design

Intervention studies are generally time-consuming and costly. They cost more than observation studies as they normally require dedicated staff to coordinate them (personnel to evaluate and recruit patients, carry out follow-up, etc.). It is even more important to clearly define the research question to be answered and to estimate how great an effect must be observed for the intervention to be deemed successful. It is not always possible, desirable, or ethical to carry out an intervention study and not all health care interventions can be assessed in this way. There must be sufficient doubt about the benefits and risks of a new intervention compared with the usual or no treatment for it to be considered ethical to allocate participants to one or other group. This important consideration is a question of clinical equipoise. Another major consideration for an intervention study is the sample size required.

Selection of study population

As with other types of study, the study or *experimental population* should be representative of the people who will ultimately receive the benefits of the intervention under trial. The experimental group will be drawn from a *reference population*, which may be limited in terms of age, sex, ethnic background, etc. As discussed previously, there is a trade-off between a study's validity and generalizability. The primary aim of a study is to produce a valid result, but intervention studies are often criticized for their lack of generalizability. For example, drug trials may be conducted on Caucasian men between 18 and 40 years of age, whereas the results are often generalized to a wider population including, for example, women and those over 40 years old.

Allocation of treatment regimens

In any intervention study, the investigators will allocate the participants either to the intervention group, which will receive the therapy or preventive action under study, or to the control group, which will receive the usual or no treatment. The two groups are then compared on outcome of interest. To avoid any underlying differences between the two groups affecting the outcome, it is important that the groups are similar in all other respects.

To ensure that bias is not introduced into these types of studies, certain safeguards have been developed. The 'gold standard' of intervention studies is the *randomized double-blind placebo-controlled trial*. In this type of study, bias is reduced in the following ways:

- Selection bias is reduced by selecting participants through randomization so that they have an equal chance of receiving the intervention.
- Measurement or reporting bias is reduced by a process called *blinding*, which avoids the investigators or the study participants finding out which treatment they have been allocated, since this can affect how they behave in the trial, and how patient outcomes are assessed.
- By ensuring that the control group is as similar to the intervention group as possible. This is often achieved by allocating the use of the usual or a dummy intervention (or *placebo*), so ensuring that the differences between the groups are due to the intervention itself and not the fact that one group is in receipt of an intervention.

In order to avoid *selection bias* when allocating study participants to intervention and control groups, the aim is to ensure that the groups are similar to each other in all respects, apart from the receipt of the intervention. If the allocation process has been performed properly, the two groups should be very similar in terms of all baseline factors that might be included in the analysis (age, sex, ethnic group, disease grade, geographic location, etc.) and hence similar in all known confounding characteristics.

It is very important that those responsible for recruiting people into an intervention study are unaware of the group to which a participant will be allocated. This avoids both conscious and unconscious selection of patients into the study. For instance, if an investigator has control over the allocation process, and knows to which treatment a patient is being assigned, they might be inclined to allocate more seriously affected patients to the treatment and less severely affected patients to the control group. One method of allocation that is particularly prone to this type of bias is *systematic allocation*, where participants are allocated to each group alternately or on alternate days, as it is easy to guess the allocation schedule.

It should be noted, however, that not all intervention studies are randomized controlled trials. Although randomized controlled trials are considered the gold standard, they are not always feasible or possible to conduct.

True randomization is the only way to limit bias in allocating a study intervention and should rely on a mechanism that is beyond the control of the investigator or the participant. This process should also be carried out once the participant has been determined eligible for inclusion and after they have consented to participate in the trial.

Allocation concealment ensures that there can be no manipulation on the part of the investigators. For single-centre trials, it may be possible to use sealed envelopes for the allocation of patients, that are not opened until a suitable participant has given consent to be entered into the trial. For multicentre clinical trials, central randomization by telephone, interactive voice response system, fax or the Internet is ideal for allocation concealment. The clinician or data manager at the participating site assesses eligibility, gains consent, and makes the decision to enrol a patient, then calls the randomization service to get the treatment allocation. Central randomization also enables trial coordinators to monitor randomization rates, and to keep a record of all allocated patients for potential follow-up.

The simplest method of randomization is by tossing a coin or using a computer to randomly allocate patients to groups (ideally, the patient and the investigator should not be aware which group has the intervention). This is known as *blinding* or *masking*. However, this method can result in groups of different sizes – you can try this for yourself by tossing a coin 20 times.

It is preferable that the comparison groups should be similar in size. One way to avoid different sized groups is to use *blocked randomization*, whereby the allocation list ensures that for every ten participants, for example, five will be in group A and five in group B. The block sequence is then randomly changed each time. The investigator should not know the block size, since they might be able to predict the allocation for the last few participants in each block.

Stratified randomization is another method used to help balance groups. It is used to ensure that characteristics that are thought to be associated with the outcome or response to the intervention are equally distributed. For example, if it is known that the effectiveness of an intervention might be influenced by age or sex, stratified randomization would ensure that these characteristics are in equal proportions in each group.

Once randomization has been completed, the success of the randomization procedure should be checked by comparing baseline factors between the two groups to ensure they are similar. If randomization is carried out correctly, it is likely that the groups will be similar in terms of all known and unknown factors.

Efficacy and effectiveness

When designing an intervention study, the investigators need to decide whether they are interested in the efficacy or the effectiveness of the intervention under study.

Efficacy refers to the effect of the intervention under trial conditions, and in such a trial the investigators would determine the maximum benefit that could be achieved by the intervention under ideal conditions. Participants would probably be a highly selected group and receive more monitoring and more encouragement to stick to their allocated treatment than might occur in clinical practice.

In an *effectiveness* trial, the aim would be to determine the effect of the intervention in routine clinical practice. The investigators might therefore expect the intervention to appear less effective than in an efficacy trial, but the results would be more generalizable to usual clinical situations and would provide a better estimate of the impact of the intervention when administered to the general population.

Other types of study design

We have mentioned that intervention studies can be carried out at the individual or group level. An example of a group-level study would be a *cluster-randomized trial*, in which groups of people, or even entire communities, are randomly assigned to the intervention or control groups. This is usually done if the intervention has an effect at group level, or when it is not feasible to randomize individuals. For example, in a study to assess an intervention that reduces air pollution, the intervention would need to be introduced at the community level since it would be impossible to introduce pollution controls at an individual level.

Another example would be educational intervention trials. It might not be feasible to allocate interventions to individuals due to *contamination* between the intervention and control groups (i.e. participants may share information which could dilute the true measure of effectiveness). For example, in a trial to assess the effectiveness of health education leaflets to promote healthy diet in school children, the investigators might randomize at the school level. If they had randomized at the individual level, children within a particular school might show the leaflets to friends in the control group, thus causing contamination of the control group.

As with any study carried out at the group level, the analysis and interpretation must reflect this. Cluster-randomized controlled trials have to have larger sample sizes to compensate for the power lost due to randomization at a group rather than an individual level.

Measuring the outcome

As mentioned above, measurement (or reporting bias) can be minimized by blinding trial investigators and participants to the allocated treatment. If both the investigator and participant are blinded, the study is referred to as *double-blind*. If it is either the participant or the investigator that is blinded, the study is *single-blind*.

Sometimes it is not possible to keep the allocation of the intervention hidden from the participant or the investigator. For example, if the study is to compare the effect of mosquito nets versus antimalarial tablets, then the participants will know which intervention they are receiving, although it might still be possible to keep the allocation of groups from the microscopists who analyse the blood samples. Alternatively, in a study to compare different surgical treatments of inguinal hernia, the surgeons will know which intervention the patients received, but it might be possible to keep the patients blind as to the exact technique used.

Placebos can be used to help the blinding process by making the intervention and control groups as similar as possible. The aim of a placebo is to make sure that the patient does not know whether they are receiving treatment or not, since it is known that simply receiving treatment can have a psychological effect on whether the patient recovers, irrespective of whether the drug actually works. This works best when the intervention is simply a pill that can be disguised. However, patients can sometimes tell whether they are receiving the intervention drug because of the side effects that they experience. Some sophisticated placebos can even mimic the side effects of the true drug, although investigators always have to remember that these side effects can also mean that patients may want to stop taking the treatment and drop out of the trial. It is not therefore always ethical to use placebos. If there is another invention available against which the new intervention could be compared, then the alternative intervention should be used as a comparison in place of a placebo.

Analysis

The main effect measures derived from intervention studies are risk ratios and rate ratios. It is also possible to calculate the attributable risk and the population attributable risk (see Chapter 3).

The main method of analysis of an intervention study should be by *intention to treat*. This means that the analysis should include results from all study participants by the groups to which they were allocated at the start of the study, even if they swapped groups or subsequently dropped out of the study. This method avoids potential biases that can arise from different levels of participation, and also because non-participants are usually different from those who complete a study in terms of their risk of side effects. It also ensures that the study is relevant to the 'real world', since if only individuals who complete their treatment are included in the analysis, the study will not necessarily be an accurate representation of what will happen when the intervention is used in the general population, in whom compliance is rarely, if ever, 100%. It is of course possible to analyse a study for only those who receive and complete their treatment regimen, but this should always be clearly stated when the results of the study are reported.

Interpretation

Once the results have been analysed, the investigators need to decide whether the results are wholly due to the intervention or whether they could be explained by other factors. If the trial has been carried out correctly, and the randomization and blinding procedures are effective, then there should be few problems with bias and confounding. It is important to distinguish between results that are statistically significant and those that are clinically significant. It may be that a result has reached statistical significance but because of other factors such as drug side effects, other adverse events and costs of implementation the treatment of interest may not be seen as a viable alternative to the next best treatment.

Ethical issues

Ethical considerations are important in intervention studies because the investigators have control over the participants and the inventions they receive. For this reason, the World Health Organization and other national and international bodies have drawn up guidelines for this type of research based on the *Declaration of Helsinki*. However, whether a study is judged to be ethical can vary greatly between countries and over time, as scientific knowledge and cultural norms develop.

Inherent to any intervention study is the fact that a group of participants are being actively denied an intervention that may be of benefit to them. Of course, if the study is a success, then the ultimate benefit will be to the general population. There is therefore the potential for many people to benefit from the fact that a few did not receive the drug in the trial, and, should results be favourable, those who participated in the trial will not continue to be denied the drug once the trial is over. Nevertheless, safeguards should be put in place to make sure that those who participated did not do so in vain.

Intervention studies need to address questions of sufficient importance to health to warrant this type of study in the first place. Studies need to be designed in such a way that they can provide the most accurate answer possible. The research question should also not already have been answered by another study, since to deny participants an established intervention would be unethical. However, it is often important to establish whether the effects of an intervention known to work on a particular group of people will work on a population with different characteristics, in different health care systems with different resources and structures.

Before participants are recruited into a trial, it is important that they are fully aware of what the study is about, what it is for and what the potential risks are. Participants then need to give their consent to participate. This is known as *informed consent*. Sometimes it is not possible for the participant to provide their consent. For example, if the intervention is a childhood vaccine, then consent will need to be sought from the parent or guardian of the child; and if the intervention is a drug that is hoped to improve the recovery of patients with severe head injuries, then it is likely that consent will be required from a close relative or guardian. Whatever form of consent is obtained, it should always be clearly stated when the results of the trial are reported.

It is also important that trial participants are allowed to refuse to participate and have the option to drop out of the trial at any time during the study. As with any study, the identity of the trial participants should be kept confidential and their privacy respected.

Strengths and weaknesses

Randomized controlled trials are considered to be the 'gold standard' of epidemiological studies and have many major advantages. Their main advantage is that they carry less risk of bias and confounding than other epidemiological studies, and can provide strong evidence of causal relationships between the intervention and the outcome. If properly randomized, and of a large enough sample size, the intervention and control groups will be similar in all respects except the intervention. If there is allocation concealment so that investigators cannot modify the randomization process selection bias and confounding will be minimized. If the investigators are blind to the treatment allocation of the participants, reporting bias and observer bias will be minimized when evaluating the patients' outcomes. If the participants themselves are blind to which intervention they received (e.g. if a placebo was given) then this can reduce responder bias.

How much these biases affect the results does depend on the outcome being evaluated. If the outcome is a particular disease or death then outcome measurement bias would not affect the results; however, if it is more subjective, such as a quality-of-life score, or reporting of side effects, then knowledge of which group participants are allocated to could affect the reporting of these outcomes. Intervention studies are similar to cohort studies in that they can be used to study multiple outcomes and can measure the incidence rate of the outcome.

However, randomized controlled trials are often expensive to carry out. They may require a large study team, in several locations, and they often need a long follow-up period. In some situations, intervention studies may be impossible to carry out because of ethical concerns. For example, if a treatment or intervention is already routinely used and there is no viable alternative, it would not be ethical to withdraw that treatment from the participants randomized to the control group, even if the effectiveness of the treatment was unknown or in doubt.

It is not uncommon for results of randomized controlled trials and non-randomized studies to be conflicting. In fact results can differ between studies of the same design. Where there is conflicting evidence from several studies, in order to provide a clearer answer, it would be necessary to assess their quality, and it may be possible to gather together in a literature review or *meta-analysis* evidence from all studies that have been conducted. It is possible, however, (and common) that no definitive answer can be reached on the available evidence.

While it is important not to base clinical practice on one study alone, there are many intervention studies that have helped changed clinical practice. A historic trial, the first truly randomized trial to be reported, established the superiority of the drug streptomycin over a period of bed rest (standard treatment at the time) for pulmonary tuberculosis (Medical Research Council Streptomycin in Tuberculosis Trials Committee 1948).

✏ Activity 8.1

A (fictitious) study was carried out in all 80,000 infants born in country X in 2002 (January to December). Infants were eligible for inclusion in the study when they were presented at a health centre aged 1 month. Parents consented for their infants to be enrolled in the study to test the vaccine efficacy of a pneumococcal vaccination.

Infants born on odd-numbered days formed the vaccine group and received the pneumococcal vaccination vaccine at 3, 4, 6 and 14 months along with the other routinely administered vaccines. Children born on even-numbered days constituted the control group and received only the routine vaccines at 3, 4, 6 and 14 months. All infants were followed up for immediate side effects and for episodes of infections for 1 year.

The children in the two treatment groups were not compared in terms of their characteristics at study entry, but were found to have similar vaccine coverage rates (approximately 98%) and similarly low rates of side effects. The pre-vaccination and post-vaccination mean antibody titre was compared in 100 of the children, although the investigators did not say how they selected this group of children. The incidence of pneumococcal disease was compared between the vaccine and control groups.

1   What sort of study is this?

2   Discuss the potential limitations of this study.

3   The pre- and post-vaccination antibody titres in the 100 children investigated in this study are given in Table 8.1. Comment on these results. Can you conclude that the new vaccine is efficacious in preventing pneumococcal disease?

Table 8.1 Pre- and post-vaccination antibody titres

Age of child (months)	Number of doses received	Number of children examined	Mean antibody titre (µg/ml)	Number of children with >2-fold rise in antibody titre
3	0	150	0.12	
4	1	147	0.15	0
6	2	143	0.13	15 (10.5%)
7	3	140	0.39	109 (77.9%)

During the first 6 months of the follow-up, 14 cases of pneumococcal disease were identified, 2 cases in the vaccine group and 12 cases in the control group.

4   Assuming that there were 40,000 children in each group, calculate the risk ratio of invasive pneumococcal infection.

5   What proportion of the expected cases of invasive pneumococcal infections seem to have been prevented by this vaccine? (Calculate the *preventable fraction*, also known as the *vaccine efficacy* – see Chapter 3.)

⟳ **Feedback**

Your answers to the questions should be along the lines of the following:

1 This is an open (non-blinded), non-randomized, controlled field trial.

2 There are three potential limitations of this study.

Method of allocation of comparison groups: Since the allocation to vaccine and control groups depended on the date of birth, parents and the physicians who followed up the children (for side effects and pneumococcal disease) could not be blind to the comparison groups. However, it is unlikely that children born on odd-numbered days are intrinsically different from those born on even-numbered days, so the two groups would be comparable in their baseline characteristics.

Selection bias: The proportion of parents refusing to participate in the study and loss to follow-up could be different between the comparison groups, depending on the perception of parents regarding the safety and efficacy of the new vaccine. This would limit the generalizability of the results.

Information bias: Physicians could overdiagnose pneumococcal disease in the control group since they knew the vaccine status of children. Similarly, the frequency of consultation by parents for symptoms suggestive of pneumococcal infection could differ between the groups. However, this is unlikely since pneumococcal infection leads to severe disease and almost all children with severe illness would be brought to a health facility in country X; also, the diagnosis of pneumococcal disease can be confirmed by bacteriological and serological investigations. However, the incidence of side effects of the vaccine could be overestimated since parents of children from the vaccine group are more likely to report to the health centre with minor side effects such as rashes.

3 There was no increase in the mean antibody titres after the first and second dose of the vaccine. However, there was a marked increase in the mean antibody titre after the third dose of the vaccine. The proportion of children with at least a two-fold increase in the antibody level jumped from 11% after two doses to 78% after three doses. It seems that for three doses of the vaccine there is a substantial immunogenic response. However, since the antibody titre can rise as a result of naturally occurring pneumococcal infections, it is difficult to assess the role of natural infection on the observed rise in the antibody titre in the vaccinated children. It would have been more informative if data on the antibody titres in a group of unvaccinated children were available for comparison. Furthermore, the risk of exposure to natural pneumococcal infection increases with age and the number of doses of vaccine increased with age. Thus, the observed increase in the antibody titre after three doses could be confounded by age. However, the fact that there is no evidence of any increase in the antibody levels until 6 months and then a sudden increase between 6 and 7 months within a month after the third dose makes it unlikely that the observed immunogenic effect of the vaccine after three doses is confounded by age. Is this observation generalizable to all children participating in this study? No information is given as to how the 150 children were selected. If they were selected randomly, they would be a representative sample of this study population, and thus it would be reasonable to conclude that this vaccine had a good immune response among children from country X.

Investigating immune response to a vaccine is necessary but is not sufficient to establish whether or not the vaccine is efficacious in preventing disease. It is possible that a vaccine can be highly immunogenic but not efficacious in the prevention of disease. To establish the vaccine efficacy, the incidence of mortality, morbidity and side effects must be compared between the vaccinated and unvaccinated children.

4 The risk ratio is calculated by dividing the risk of disease in those who were vaccinated by the risk of disease in those who were unvaccinated:

$$\text{Risk ratio} = \frac{2/40{,}000}{12/40{,}000} = \frac{2}{12} = 0.1667.$$

5 Preventable fraction (or vaccine efficacy) can be calculated by either of the following methods:

$$\text{Vaccine efficacy} = \frac{\text{Incidence in unvaccinated} - \text{Incidence in vaccinated}}{\text{Incidence in unvaccinated}}$$

$$= \frac{(12/40{,}000) - (2/40{,}000)}{(12/40{,}000)} = 0.8333 = 83\%$$

or

$$\text{Vaccine efficacy} = 1 - \text{Risk ratio} = 1 - 0.1667 = 0.8333 = 83\%.$$

Summary

In this chapter you have learned about the key features of intervention studies. You should now be able to describe the features of an intervention study, understand their strengths and limitations, and be able to discuss the associated ethical and policy issues.

Reference

Medical Research Council Streptomycin in Tuberculosis Trials Committee (1948) Streptomycin treatment for pulmonary tuberculosis. *British Medical Journal* ii: 769–82.

9

Interpretation of the results of epidemiological studies

Overview

Most epidemiological studies aim to identify exposures that may increase or decrease the risk of developing a certain disease (or outcome). Unfortunately, errors in the design, conduct and analysis can distort the results of any epidemiological study, including randomized controlled trials. Even if errors do not seem to be an obvious explanation for an observed association between an exposure and an outcome, it may or may not be causal. In this chapter, you will learn more about the potential pitfalls in epidemiological studies and the steps involved in interpreting an observed association between an exposure and an outcome.

Learning objectives

After working through this session, you will be better able to:

- **discuss the different types of bias that can distort the results of epidemiological studies**
- **understand that a confounding variable provides an alternative explanation for an observed association between an exposure and an outcome**
- **understand the role of chance**
- **describe the steps involved in determining whether or not an association between an exposure and an outcome is causal.**

Key terms

Random error The variation of an observed value from the true population value due to chance alone.

How do we interpret the results of a study?

The aim of most epidemiological studies is to establish causal association between risk factors (exposure) and disease (or other outcome) so that preventive measures can be taken to limit the morbidity and mortality of the disease. In the previous chapters on epidemiological study designs, you learned how the results of a study are analysed. For example, you can calculate a measure of relative risk for an association between a risk factor and disease. However, before we can conclude that an observed association is causal (i.e. that the risk factor really does cause disease), we first need to exclude all other possible reasons why we might have obtained that result.

First, we need to ask whether the association was due to errors in the way the study was conducted. This includes the way in which study participants were selected and how information was obtained from them. As you will recall from previous chapters, this is known as bias.

Secondly, were there any differences between the groups in terms of other variables that were not measured or taken into account in the analysis? These factors are known as confounders.

Thirdly, could the observed association be due to chance?

A study's *internal validity* relates to how well the study is designed to ensure that the findings are not a result of or affected by chance, bias and confounding. Once we have ruled out all of these possible reasons, we can then ask whether the association is likely to be *causal*. However, this still depends on several important criteria being met.

Bias

In previous chapters we have mentioned some of the ways in which bias can occur in study design and measurement of an association. Here, we give an overview of bias in the study designs you have met. Bias can be categorized into two classes:

- selection bias
- information bias (or measurement bias).

Selection bias

Selection bias occurs when systematic errors are introduced by the selection of study participants or allocation of individuals to different study groups. These errors can compromise the (internal) validity of results of a study. This can occur if the participants selected for the study are not representative of the general population to which the study will ultimately apply, or if the comparison groups are not comparable (case–control or intervention studies). For example, if subjects are allowed to choose between a new drug that is being tested and an established drug, the more adventurous or health-conscious individuals might like to try the new drug, whereas the less adventurous or less well-informed individuals may opt for the established drug. Differences in the effects of the two drugs observed in such a study design may be partly or entirely due to the differences in the underlying characteristics of the study participants rather than in the effects of the drugs. For these reasons it is preferable to randomly assign participants to the study drug or control in intervention studies.

In case–control studies, selection bias can occur in the selection of cases if they are not representative of all cases within the population, or in the selection of controls if they are not representative of the population that produced the cases.

In cohort studies, selection bias may occur if the exposed and unexposed groups are not truly comparable. This might happen if the unexposed group is not correctly selected, and differs from the exposed groups in other, unrelated, factors in addition to the exposure of interest. An example of this would be comparing an occupational cohort with the general population. Any association with the exposure and disease might be lost due to the *healthy worker effect*. Bias may also occur if there are differences in follow-up between the comparison groups. For example, an occupational cohort may be much easier to follow up for longer periods of time than the general population, which may lead to more accurate and complete data being collected in the exposed group.

Information bias

Information (or measurement) bias occurs if an inaccurate measurement or classification of an outcome or exposure is made. This could mean that individuals are assigned to the wrong exposure or outcome category, and will then result in an incorrect estimation of the association between exposure and outcome. Errors in measurement are also known as *misclassifications*, and might be introduced by the observer (observer bias), by the study participants (recall bias), or by the measurement tools such as weighing scales or questionnaires.

The size and direction of the distortion of an observed association between an exposure and an outcome depends on the type of misclassification, of which there are two types:

* differential misclassification
* non-differential (random) misclassification.

Only differential misclassification leads to information bias, although we will discuss both types of misclassification here for completeness.

Differential misclassification

Differential misclassification occurs when one group of participants is more likely to be misclassified than the other. In a cohort study differential misclassification can occur if exposure makes the individuals more or less likely to be classified as having the disease. In a case–control study, differential misclassification can occur if cases are more or less likely to be classified as being exposed than controls.

Differential misclassification can therefore lead to an over- or underestimation of an association between exposure and outcome. We will illustrate this in the next activity.

✏ Activity 9.1

In a case–control study designed to investigate the association between the use of oral contraceptives and ovarian cancer, the exposure to oral contraceptives was determined from the history given by the study participants. Cases are women diagnosed with ovarian cancer and controls are those who do not have ovarian cancer. The investigators assume that women with ovarian cancer are more likely to recall the use of oral contraceptives than those who do not have the cancer.

1   Do you think differential misclassification is likely to occur?

2   If so, how do you think it would affect the observed effect of use of contraceptives on ovarian cancer?

Table 9.1 shows the odds of exposure to contraceptives in cases and controls in the study.

Table 9.1 Odds of exposure to oral contraceptives in cases and controls

Exposure	Cases	Controls
Oral contraceptive users	40	50
Oral contraceptive non-users	60	50
Total	100	100

3   What is the actual odds ratio of exposure to contraceptives in cases compared to controls?

Suppose that the cases recalled the use of oral contraceptives accurately, but the controls did not (scenario 1). This could lead to the results shown in Table 9.2.

Table 9.2 Observed odds of exposure in scenario 1

Exposure	Cases	Controls
Oral contraceptive users	40	30
Oral contraceptive non-users	60	70
Total	100	100

4   What is the observed odds ratio of exposure to contraceptives in cases compared to controls in scenario 1?

 Feedback

Your answers should be along the following lines:

1 Yes, differential misclassification is likely to occur because the probability of misclassification differs between the case group and the control group.

2 Here, the protective effect of use of oral contraceptives would be underestimated since the odds of exposure to oral contraceptives are likely to be overestimated or correctly estimated among cases whereas it will be underestimated among the controls.

3 The odds of exposure to contraceptives are 40/60 in the cases and 50/50 in the controls. Therefore, the odds ratio of exposure to contraceptives among cases compared to controls is calculated as follows:

$$\text{Odds ratio} = \frac{40/60}{50/50} = \frac{40 \times 50}{50 \times 60} = 0.67.$$

4 Since all the cases who had used contraceptives were able to recall accurately, there was no misclassification of exposure to contraceptives among the cases. However, 40% of controls who had actually used contraceptives failed to recall the use of contraceptives and this led to an underestimation of odds of exposure to contraceptives among the controls. Therefore, the observed odds ratio of exposure to contraceptives among cases compared to the controls is:

$$\text{Odds ratio} = \frac{40/60}{30/70} = \frac{40 \times 70}{30 \times 60} = 1.6,$$

which is clearly an overestimate of the actual odds ratio. In other words, this *biased* estimate suggests that use of oral contraceptives is a risk factor rather than a protective factor for ovarian cancer.

Non-differential misclassification

Non-differential misclassification occurs when both groups (cases or controls, exposed or unexposed) are equally likely to be misclassified. This form of misclassification is therefore *independent* of exposure status or outcome status. Non-differential misclassification usually leads to underestimation of an association between exposure and outcome, and will therefore reduce the observed strength of the association.

Suppose that, in the case–control study discussed above, the exposure to oral contraceptives was determined from the records of family planning clinics. It is likely that the records of some women might not be traceable. However, the loss of records would probably be distributed equally among the cases and the controls, since record-keeping in family planning clinics is independent of the risk of women developing cancer. If the investigators decided to classify all women who did not have a record in the family planning clinics as unexposed to contraceptives, then the odds of exposure to contraceptives would be underestimated in both cases and controls. Although the odds of exposure to contraceptives would be underestimated equally among cases and controls, it would lead to underestimation of the effect of contraceptives on ovarian cancer.

Activity 9.2

Continuing with the study considered in Activity 9.1, suppose now that the records of 40% of both the cases and the controls who had used oral contraceptives were not traced and these subjects were misclassified as non-users (scenario 2). The observed odds of exposure in scenario 2 are shown in Table 9.3.

What is the observed odds ratio of exposure to contraceptives in cases compared to controls in scenario 2?

Table 9.3 Observed odds of exposure in scenario 2

Exposure	Cases	Controls
Oral contraceptive users	24	30
Oral contraceptive non-users	76	70
Total	100	100

 Feedback

The odds of exposure to contraceptives among cases is 24/76 and among controls is 30/70. Although the proportions of cases and controls misclassified are equal (40%), the odds ratio of exposure to contraceptives among cases compared to controls is underestimated:

$$\text{Odds ratio} = \frac{24/76}{30/70} = \frac{24 \times 70}{30 \times 76} = 0.74.$$

Avoiding information bias

Information bias can be minimized either in the study design or in the way in which data are collected. Blinding can be used to prevent recall bias and observer bias. This need not apply just to intervention studies. For example, in case–control studies those who are determining the exposure status of a study participant should be unaware of whether the latter is a case or a control. Blinding of study participants may be more difficult, but sometimes this is done by not revealing the exact research question.

With data collection, the best way to avoid bias is to use objective records rather than relying on recall, and to use automated measuring devices rather than relying on observers. Data on exposures should also be collected as near as possible to the time of exposure.

If questionnaires are used, then good questionnaire design is essential. Questionnaires need to be valid and reliable. A questionnaire's *validity* relates to how well the questions measure what they are supposed to measure. The validity of a questionnaire could be established by cross-referencing answers to a question with a gold standard. Often studies can use questionnaires that have already been validated, such as quality-of-life questionnaires. Ideally questions should be closed (have a limited number of possible answers), specific and unambiguous. A questionnaire's *reliability* relates to the likelihood of obtaining similar results if the questionnaire were to be repeated, or, if answers are different, the proportion of these differences are due to *true* differences and what proportion are due random errors. Interviewers should be trained to ask questions in the same way, and should also be blind to the exposure status of the participant (if possible). Streiner and Norman (2003) give practical guidance on questionnaire design.

Confounding

Confounding provides an alternative explanation for an association between an exposure and an outcome. It occurs when an observed association between an exposure and an outcome is distorted because the exposure of interest is correlated with another risk factor. This additional risk factor is also associated with the outcome, but independently of the exposure of interest. An unequal distribution of this additional risk factor between those who are exposed and unexposed will result in confounding.

This situation is illustrated in Figure 9.1. Here, association 1 is an example of confounding where smoking is the confounding variable in a study to assess the relationship between occupation and lung cancer. In association 2, the variable blood cholesterol is on the causal pathway between diet and heart disease, is not associated with the disease independently of diet, and is therefore not a confounder. In association 3, alcohol consumption is not a confounder because it is not associated with lung cancer at all.

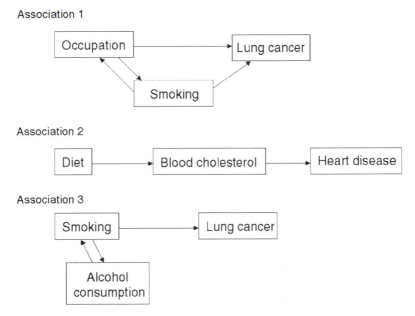

Figure 9.1 Associations

A potential confounder is any factor that can have an effect on the risk of disease under study. This includes factors that have direct causal links with the disease, and factors that are proxy measures for other unknown causes (i.e. age and social class). Remember that you encountered age as a confounder in Chapter 2, when you calculated standardized mortality ratios.

In the next activity, you will look at the effect that confounding can have on the estimates of association calculated in a study.

Activity 9.3

In a case–control study, coffee drinking was observed to be associated with the risk of cancer of the pancreas. The importance of this association was disputed because it was noted that coffee drinking was correlated with cigarette smoking and cigarette smoking was also associated with cancer of the pancreas. So, cigarette smoking may have confounded the observed association between coffee drinking and cancer of the pancreas. The observed odds of exposure to coffee among all cases and controls are shown in Table 9.4.

Table 9.4 Odds of exposure to coffee among all cases and controls

Exposure	Cases	Controls	Total
Coffee drinkers	450	600	1 050
Non-coffee drinkers	300	750	1 050
Total	750	1 350	2 100

1   What is the odds ratio of exposure to coffee in cases compared to controls?

Because the researchers in this study believed that coffee drinking and cigarette smoking might be correlated, and also that cigarette smoking was associated with cancer of the pancreas, they calculated the odds ratio of exposure among smokers and non-smokers separately (Table 9.5).

Table 9.5 Odds of exposure to coffee in cases and controls stratified by exposure to smoking

Exposure	Smokers		Non-smokers		Total
	Cases	Controls	Cases	Controls	
Coffee drinkers	400	300	50	300	1 050
Non-coffee drinkers	200	150	100	600	1 050
Total	600	450	150	900	2 100

2   What is the odds ratio of exposure to coffee compared to controls among smokers and non-smokers?

3   What is your inference regarding the association between coffee drinking and cancer of the pancreas?

To explore confounding further, look at the evidence of association between smoking and coffee drinking, and between smoking and cancer of the pancreas as shown in Tables 9.6 and 9.7.

Table 9.6 Association between smoking and coffee drinking

Exposure	Smokers	Non-smokers	Total
Coffee drinkers	700	350	1 050
Non-coffee drinkers	350	700	1 050
Total	1 050	1 050	2 100

Table 9.7 Association between smoking and cancer of the pancreas

Exposure	Cases	Controls	Total
Smokers	600	450	1 050
Non-smokers	150	900	1 050
Total	750	1 350	2 100

4 What is the odds ratio of coffee drinking among smokers compared to non-smokers?

5 What is the odds ratio of smoking in cases compared controls?

 Feedback

1 Odds of exposure in cases = 450/300 and odds of exposure in controls = 600/750.

$$\text{Odds ratio of exposure to coffee} = \frac{450/300}{600/750} = 1.9.$$

2 Odds ratio of exposure to coffee in cases compared to controls among smokers = $\frac{400/200}{300/150} = 1.0.$

Odds ratio of exposure to coffee in cases compared to controls among non-smokers = $\frac{50/100}{300/600} = 1.0.$

3 Although the crude odds ratio was 1.9, when stratified according to exposure to smoking the odds ratio of exposure to coffee drinking is 1.0 in both smokers and non-smokers. This shows that the observed association between coffee drinking and cancer of the pancreas is confounded by the effect of smoking.

4 Odds ratio of coffee drinking among smokers compared to non-smokers = $\frac{700/350}{350/700}$ = 4.0.

This shows that smokers are 4 times as likely to drink coffee as non-smokers.

5 Odds ratio of smoking in cases compared to controls = $\frac{600/150}{450/900} = 8.0.$

This shows that individuals with cancer of the pancreas are 8 times as likely as healthy controls to be smokers. Since smoking is strongly associated with cancer of the pancreas and is also associated with coffee drinking, it is not surprising that smoking was confounding the observed association between coffee drinking and cancer of the pancreas.

Control of confounding

Confounding can be dealt with at the study design stage or in the analysis, as long as data on potential confounders have been collected. There are three ways to deal with confounding at the design stage: restriction, randomization, and matching.

Restriction simply limits the study to include people who are similar in relation to the confounder. For example, if sex is known to be a confounder, the study may be designed only to include men. However, this does then mean that the results of that study can only be applied to men.

Randomization is the best method to control for confounding, because it helps to ensure that known (and even unknown) confounding variables are distributed evenly between the study groups. However, this method can only be used in intervention studies (Chapter 8).

Matching is usually only used in case–control studies and ensures that controls are selected who are similar to cases in terms of potential confounders (Chapter 7).

At the analysis stage, there are two further methods available for controlling confounders. The first is *stratification*, which can be thought of as an extension of restriction. However, rather than only studying people who are similar in relation to the confounder, the confounding variable can be split into groups (e.g. men and women), and associations between exposure and outcome analysed separately in each group. However, a problem with stratification in the analysis of any study design is that the more the original sample is stratified the smaller the sample size of each subsample becomes, and hence the power to detect associations is reduced.

Another method, which does not have the same problems of loss of power, is to use statistical modelling techniques, whereby data on potential confounders are included in the statistical model, which then simultaneously adjusts for all confounding variables. This is often used in cohort studies.

Stratification and statistical modelling are techniques usually carried out on non-randomized studies, as in randomized studies patient characteristics should be equally distributed in each group.

Role of chance

Generally, epidemiological studies are limited to a sample of individuals from a reference population because it is usually impractical to include all individuals. However, based on the estimates observed in the sample population, it is possible to make inferences about the actual risk in the reference population. For example, to assess the coverage of immunization in a community, researchers may study the immunization status in a random sample of 210 children and extrapolate the observed coverage to all children in that community. However, observed estimates from samples of individuals will differ in other samples of individuals from the same community.

Statistical methods can be used to assess the probability of obtaining an observed estimate in a sample by chance alone, and to assess the range of values within which the actual estimate is likely to fall.

We will give only a brief explanation of the P-values obtained from statistical significance tests and of confidence intervals.

P-values

A P-value obtained from a statistical significance test gives the probability of obtaining an observed estimate by chance. For example, if you did a significance test for the association between oral contraceptives and ovarian cancer shown in Table 9.1 (odds ratio = 0.67), the resulting P-value would be 0.20.

A P-value of 0.20 tells you that the probability of obtaining the odds ratio of 0.67 in this sample by chance is 0.20 (i.e. 1 in 5). Since a 1 in 5 chance is fairly high, the observed odds ratio of 0.67 is likely to have occurred by chance. Conventionally, if the P-value is less than 0.05 (i.e. the probability of obtaining the observed estimate by chance is less than 1 in 20), then the role of chance in obtaining the observed result is rejected, and the calculated estimate can be interpreted as a significant estimate for that association.

Confidence intervals

If you calculate the 95% confidence interval for the odds ratio for Table 9.1, you get the range 0.37–1.21. This tells us that the probability that the true odds ratio falls outside this range is 1 in 20. In this example, the range of the 95% confidence interval goes from less than 1.0 (indicating that the exposure is protective) to more than 1.0 (indicating that the exposure is a risk factor). This suggests that the odds ratio is not significantly different from 1.0 (indicating no significant association between exposure and outcome). If a 95% confidence interval was small and the entire range was less than 1.0, you might be confident in extrapolating the observed estimate of 0.67 to the reference population. Conversely, if the interval is large, or includes 1.0, you should be cautious in extrapolating the observed estimate.

Activity 9.4

In each of the following examples, the association between the exposure and the outcome has arisen as a result of error. For each example, identify which type of error has occurred (bias, confounding, or random error) and write down why you think it occurred (imagine you are explaining your reasons to a colleague).

1   In a study of risk factors for infant mortality, it is found that infant mortality is significantly lower in households where the father wears a silk tie. The investigators therefore conclude that if silk ties were given to fathers, infant mortality would fall.

2   Four people want to give up smoking. Two of them take garlic pills to help them stop, and two do not. The two who take garlic pills succeed in giving up smoking. The other two do not. The investigators conclude that garlic pills help people give up smoking. However, a significance test shows that $P = 0.3$.

3 In a case–control study to examine risk factors for lung cancer, cases are people admitted to hospital with lung cancer, and controls are people admitted to the same hospital with emphysema (a chronic lung disease for which smoking is a risk factor). The study finds no association between smoking and lung cancer.

 Feedback

1 Here the error is confounding. Low socioeconomic group is a risk factor for infant mortality. Here the exposure of interest is wearing a silk tie, which is associated with socioeconomic group. So the apparent association between wearing a silk tie and lower infant mortality is due to confounding with socioeconomic group. Socioeconomic group (the confounder) is an alternative explanation for the apparent association between wearing of a silk tie (the exposure of interest) and infant mortality (the outcome).

2 In this example the result was due to chance or random error. This study shows an apparent association between taking garlic pills and giving up smoking, but the number of subjects is very small, and the *P*-value is 0.3. Here the association is due to random error.

3 The study has been badly designed and has resulted in bias. The controls are more likely to be smokers than is the population that produced the cases. In an appropriate control group, the prevalence of smoking among the controls would be the same as among the population that produced the cases.

Determining a cause–effect relationship

When determining whether a relationship is causal, the first step is to rule out bias, confounding and chance as likely explanations for the observed association between an exposure and an outcome. If none of these factors explains the observed association, you can conclude that, according to these data, there is a valid association between the exposure and outcome. A valid statistical association does not, on its own, imply a causal relationship. A number of further criteria need to be considered, including the temporal sequence of the relationship, dose–response relationship, strength of the association, biological plausibility, and consistency of the finding.

Bradford Hill (1965) published a list of criteria that need to be considered when assessing whether an association is likely to be causal. These points serve as a general guide, and are not meant to be an inflexible list. Not all criteria must be fulfilled to establish scientific causation.

Temporal relationship

To be causal, the suspected factor must have occurred, or have been present, before the outcome (e.g. a disease) developed. This is an essential criterion and is more complex than it may seem. It is generally easier to establish a temporal relationship in prospective studies than in cross-sectional or case–control studies where measurements of the exposure and outcome are made at the same time.

Dose–response relationship

The observation of a gradient of risk associated with the degree of exposure is commonly considered as supportive evidence for causality. For example, the fact that those who smoke a moderate number of cigarettes have a death rate from coronary heart disease between the rates observed in non-smokers and heavy smokers adds credibility to the hypothesis that smoking increases the risk of coronary heart disease. However, the presence of a dose–response relationship alone does not confirm a cause–effect relationship and conversely, the absence of a dose–response relationship does not rule out a cause–effect relationship.

Strength of association

The stronger the association (i.e. the greater the magnitude of increased or decreased risk observed), the less likely it is that the relationship is due to the effect of some uncontrolled or unsuspected confounding variable. For example, mortality from laryngeal cancer among heavy smokers might be observed to be 20 times higher than in non-smokers. To account for such a high risk by another variable associated with the risk of laryngeal cancer, the second variable would have to be present in smokers at a very much higher rate than among non-smokers. Since it is unlikely that such a factor exists, the strong association between smoking and laryngeal cancer could well be a cause–effect relationship. This line of reasoning does not imply that an association of small magnitude cannot be judged to be one of cause and effect – only that in such cases it is more difficult to exclude alternative explanations.

Biological plausibility

The notion of a cause–effect relationship is enhanced if there is a known, or postulated, biological mechanism by which the exposure might reasonably alter the risk of developing the outcome. For example, a causal interpretation of an observed association between the consumption of moderate amounts of alcohol and decreased risk of coronary heart disease is enhanced by the fact that alcohol is known to increase the level of high density lipoprotein, which is associated with a decreased risk of coronary heart disease. Since what is considered biologically plausible at any given time depends on current knowledge, the lack of a known or postulated mechanism does not necessarily rule out a cause–effect relationship. For example, John Snow postulated that water was the source of cholera epidemics in London long before the identification of *Vibrio cholera* (see Chapter 1).

Consistency with other studies

When many studies conducted by different investigators at various times using different methods in a variety of geographic and cultural settings show similar results, then we can assert that we have evidence of a cause–effect relationship. For example, the assessment of a cause–effect relationship between cigarette smoking and coronary heart disease has been enhanced by the fact that similar results have been obtained by a number of cohort and case–control studies conducted over 30 years in different populations.

Specificity

If a particular exposure increases the risk of a certain disease, but does not increase the risk of other diseases, this may be taken as evidence in favour of a cause–effect relationship. However, one-to-one relationships between exposure and disease are rare, since many diseases are the result of more than factor, and any lack of specificity should not be used to refute a potential causal relationship.

Reversibility

Does removal of a presumed cause lead to a reduction in the risk of ill health? Reduction in a particular exposure, if followed by a reduced risk of a particular disease, may strengthen the presumption of a real cause–effect relationship.

Coherence

The potential cause–effect relationship should not seriously conflict with previous knowledge of the natural history and biology of the disease.

Analogy

In addition, the causal relationship is likely to be further supported if there are analogies with other (well-established) cause–effect relationships.

✏ Activity 9.5

Several case reports of mesothelioma among workers at a factory led to a (fictitious) investigation of a possible association between exposure to asbestos and cancer mortality.

The investigators reviewed the occupation of people who had died during the study period (1992–2004) from the local vital registration system. From this review of over 100,000 death certificates, they identified 863 deaths of former factory workers (a later historical cohort study showed that the actual number of deceased workers was 3026). A team of interviewers was able to contact relatives of 402 of the deceased workers.

Exposure to asbestos was ascertained from the information given by the relatives in response to the question 'Did he (the deceased worker) work with asbestos?' If the answer was 'yes', then the deceased was classified as exposed; if the answer was 'no' or 'don't know', the deceased was classified as unexposed. The interviewers were blind to the cause of death recorded in the death certificate.

Since all deaths occurred in men, age-specific proportional mortality rates for men in 2002 were used to calculate the age-standardized expected number of all cancer deaths and mesothelioma-specific deaths among nuclear and non-nuclear workers. The results are given in Tables 9.8 and 9.9. The standardized mortality ratio (observed/ expected) was introduced in Chapter 2.

Table 9.8 Observed and expected number of cancer deaths among factory workers

Exposure	Cancer deaths		Observed/expected	P-value
	Observed	Expected		
Workers exposed to asbestos	42	21.8	1.9	<0.001
Workers not exposed	81	70.1	1.2	0.20

Table 9.9 Observed and expected number of mesothelioma deaths among factory workers

Exposure	Mesothelioma deaths		Observed/expected	P-value
	Observed	Expected		
Nuclear workers	7	1.5	4.7	<0.001
Non-nuclear workers	3	3.3	0.9	0.96

1 What do the results in Tables 9.8 and 9.9 show?

2 Discuss the possible sources of bias in this study that might have distorted the results.

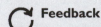 **Feedback**

Your answers to the questions should be along the lines of the following:

1 These results show a 1.9-fold excess mortality from all cancers and 4.7-fold excess mortality from mesothelioma among factory workers. These observed excess mortalities are statistically significant since the probability of obtaining these differences by chance is very low (P-value less than 0.001, i.e. less than 1 in 1000). There was no such significant excess mortality from all cancers or mesothelioma among non-nuclear workers.

2 There are two possible sources of bias in this study.

Selection bias. Only 28.5% (863/3026) of the total deaths were identified. These deaths may not be a representative sample of all deaths. For example, the registrar may have given special attention to recording the history of work at the factory for those who had died of cancer. Relatives of the deceased men were contacted for only 46.6% (402/863) of the identified deaths. The distribution of causes of death among workers whose relatives were contacted could be different from that among workers whose relatives were not contacted. For instance, it may have been easier to contact relatives of those who died of cancer because their addresses were clearly recorded for future reference purposes. On the other hand, they may have been more likely to move out of the area due to health problems.

Information bias. The relatives may not have accurately recalled the exposure status of the deceased men. For example, the relatives of men who had died of cancer were more likely to recall that the deceased worked with asbestos than the relatives of those who had died of other causes.

Summary

You should now be aware that the results of any epidemiological study have to be interpreted with caution. Although most investigators aim to get rid of bias, to control for confounding, and to rule out the role of chance, it is worthwhile reassessing these issues while interpreting and applying the results in any given situation.

You should be able to discuss the different types of bias that can distort the results of epidemiological studies.

You should also understand how a confounding variable provides an alternative explanation for an observed association between an exposure and an outcome.

You should understand the role of chance, and be able to describe the steps involved in determining whether or not an association between an exposure and an outcome is causal.

References

Bradford Hill A (1965) The environment and disease: association or causation? *Proceedings of the Royal Society of Medicine* 58: 295–300.

Streiner DL, Norman GR (2003) *Health Measurement Scales: A Practical Guide to their Development and Use* (3rd edn). Oxford: Oxford University Press.

10

Prevention strategies

Overview

Having learned about the different measures of risk in a population (relative and absolute risk), we will now discuss how different public health strategies can be used to reduce the risk of a known exposure. We will also learn about the three levels of disease prevention, described as primary, secondary and tertiary prevention. Screening for disease is a major component of secondary prevention and is discussed further in Chapter 11.

Learning objectives

After working through this chapter, you will be better able to:

- **understand the different approaches to prevention, where strategies are directed at either high risk individuals or the general population**
- **understand the terms primary, secondary and tertiary prevention.**

Preventive medicine

The aims of preventive medicine and public health strategies are to promote good health and to prevent disease. Public health professionals develop and disseminate information on behaviours that promote good health and reduce the risks of developing disease as well as on exposures that may predispose to the development of a condition.

Epidemiological studies generate and test hypotheses on the causes of disease and can provide the public and policy makers with quantitative information on the risks posed by certain behaviours and exposures. This information can be used at an individual level to improve health and reduce disease risks (e.g. an individual may adopt a low salt diet) or can form part of public health policies aimed at improving the health of whole populations (e.g. the fluoridation of water). Public health strategies can be aimed at the general population or can be targeted at those individuals considered to be in a high risk group. The differences between these two population approaches, and their advantages and disadvantages, will be discussed in this chapter.

Approaches to prevention

When we consider the prevention of disease, it is useful to use a concept first developed by Leavell and Clark (1965), which describes three levels of prevention: primary, secondary and tertiary. This concept rests on an understanding of the causes of the disease in question and knowledge of its natural history. The level of prevention used in preventive medicine or public health strategy will depend on the stage of the disease.

Primary prevention

The aim of primary prevention is to prevent a disease becoming established. It aims therefore to reduce or eliminate exposures and behaviours that are known to increase an individual's risk of developing a disease. Examples include preventing exposure to lead in the atmosphere, promoting the use of barrier contraception and avoiding exposure to tobacco smoke. When provided with information on risks, individuals can make decisions to change their lifestyle and modify a behaviour, such as decreasing weekly intake of alcohol. Primary prevention at a population level may require societal changes to support them – for example, regulating tobacco advertising, imposing taxes, or increasing the price of tobacco products. All these methods are an attempt to discourage the uptake and continued use of tobacco.

Primary prevention strategies can be aimed at the general population (e.g. promoting a healthier, low fat diet) or can be targeted at high risk groups (e.g. encouraging overweight individuals to take part in a weight loss programme). Other primary prevention strategies include childhood immunization programmes and laws to mandate the use of seat belts and motorcycle crash helmets as well as education strategies to inform the public of the risks of tobacco use.

Secondary prevention

The aim of secondary prevention is to detect early disease and to slow down or halt the progress of the disease. Once a disease has become established, it will progress until it is clinically detectable, although an individual may be asymptomatic at this stage. Knowledge of the natural history of disease can lead to the development of screening tests to detect these early stages of disease, or pre-disease states. An example is the detection of bowel polyps, which are known to develop into colorectal cancers. In the case of colorectal cancer, a high-risk secondary prevention strategy is already in place in some industrialized nations, with individuals with a family history of the disease being invited to attend screening. Another example of secondary prevention would be advice to reduce excess weight, high blood pressure or high cholesterol before clinical symptoms manifest themselves. A major component of secondary prevention is screening, which uses available tests to detect early stages of a disease process and offer treatment that will beneficially alter the natural course of the disease. Screening is discussed further in Chapter 12.

Tertiary prevention

When disease is established, detectable and symptomatic, tertiary prevention aims to reduce the complications or severity of disease by offering appropriate treatments and interventions. For example, renal disease and glaucoma, both complications of uncontrolled diabetes, may be prevented in the diabetic patient if blood glucose levels are successfully regulated through the use of insulin and/or dietary restrictions.

In summary, while primary prevention hopes to stop diseases developing in the first place, secondary and tertiary prevention strategies aim to alter the course of a disease already present, offering the patient a better outcome and quality of life.

The prevention paradox

Individuals and the general public can make decisions to modify their behaviour with respect to known risk factors in the hope of avoiding disease. The paradox of this approach, however, is that the majority are unlikely to benefit directly from this change in behaviour. An individual's decision to reduce their daily salt intake may only have a small impact on their risk of developing hypertension, but if a large proportion of the population reduce their salt intake, the community's experience of hypertension will be reduced. If a large number of individuals each reduce their risk slightly, the whole population may show a large reduction in risk, and this is often described as the *prevention paradox*.

How can a prevention strategy have little effect on the risk experienced by an individual but have a large effect on the experience of a community? We will discuss an example below to illustrate the prevention paradox.

Maternal age and risk of Down's syndrome

In some high income countries women in early pregnancy are offered prenatal screening for Down's syndrome, a congenital abnormality, after which they can make a decision whether to continue with their pregnancy.

The risk of giving birth to a baby with Down's syndrome increases rapidly with age and, until recently, it has been widely accepted that only women above a certain age would be offered the test – in other words, women for whom the individual cost of the test justifies the potential benefits. If we assumed that the screening test for this condition had high sensitivity (see Chapter 12) and was able to accurately detect a large proportion of fetuses with Down's syndrome, we would expect screening to have a significant impact on the number of babies born with Down's syndrome. However, the paradox lies in the fact that most babies with Down's are delivered by younger women, as a larger number of younger women give birth (see Table 10.1). For these younger women, the individual risk is low and the individual and social costs of screening may not justify the individual gain. The social costs of screening include the associated anxiety of undergoing medical tests, and the potential to lose the baby. The decision to terminate a pregnancy will be a very difficult one to make and, in a small proportion of cases, a false positive test will lead to the termination of a healthy fetus. When considering whether to undertake

Table 10.1 The risk of a Down's syndrome pregnancy, by maternal age

Maternal age	% of all births in the population	No. of Down's syndrome births /1000 pregnancies	% of all Down's syndrome births
Under 20	9	0.4	5
20–24	30	0.4	17
25–29	34	0.5	25
30–34	19	1.0	27
35–39	6	2.2	18
40–44	1	5.1	7
45+	0.1	8.1	1
All ages	100	0.7	100

Source: Rose (1992)

a test for Down's syndrome, the parents need to consider whether the information will change the outcome of the pregnancy.

We can see from Table 10.1 that screening older women (aged 35+) will only result in a small reduction in the number of babies born with Down's syndrome. It is for this reason that a number of screening tests, which lower the individual costs and provide an accurate prenatal diagnosis, are being considered for more widespread adoption. A tiny reduction in the risk for the majority of pregnant women may lead to a substantially lower number of babies being born with Down's syndrome. In the UK, the National Screening Committee has recommended that all pregnant women, irrespective of age, should be offered screening for Down's syndrome.

High risk strategies versus population strategies

As illustrated in the example above, a prevention strategy can be targeted at the whole population or at high risk groups. There are no quick answers to the question of which strategy to adopt, and in order to develop the most appropriate strategy we need to have an idea of the impact of the policy and how and where it might be instituted. If we consider a risk factor that is normally distributed in the population, we must ask whether it would be more beneficial to target the small proportion of the population who fall in the tails of this normal distribution, or whether to aim to improve the position of the whole population by shifting the whole distribution in the desired direction.

To analyse the potential impact of a prevention strategy, we need to examine the ability of different definitions of high risk to predict the onset of disease. In the example below, we use data from a study on the risk factors for heart disease and myocardial infarction to assess the impact of two high risk prevention strategies.

Risk factors for heart disease and heart attack

A number of factors have been identified as risk factors for heart attack (myocardial infarction (MI), including smoking, raised blood pressure, high cholesterol and psychosocial stress. We will look at data from a study which looked at three of these risk factors. The risk of MI increases with the number of risk factors to which an

Table 10.2 Predicted risk of myocardial infarction in relation to risk factors for heart disease

Exposure	Percentage of men	Percentage of men later suffering a heart attack	Percentage of all attacks occurring in this group
All men	100	4	100
Elevated risk factors	15	7	32
Elevated risk factors and early disease	2	22	12

Source: Rose (1992)

individual is exposed, and the presence of early signs of disease (see Table 10.2). If a prevention strategy focused on individuals with elevated risk factors, only 15% of men would qualify.

Follow-up of the cohort in this study showed that only 7% of the men with elevated risk factors developed an MI, with 93% remaining well. This tells us that if high risk is defined broadly, most individuals will not go on to develop the outcome of interest.

If the definition of high risk included individuals with exposure to risk factors and the signs of early heart disease, although the risk of death from MI is higher (22%), the data suggest that only 12% of MIs occur in this group and so 88% of MIs would not be prevented.

As the vast majority of MIs occur in men who do not appear to be in a high risk group, in this case a primary prevention strategy would be aimed at the whole population, attempting to shift the distribution towards the lower levels of all identified risk factors. Using the data in this study, we can see that up to 68% of MIs occur in men who do not have either exposure to risk factors or signs of early disease. If all efforts were focused only on these high risk men, even if prevention was 100% effective, the public health impact would be small. If a population-wide strategy were put into place and all men over a certain age modified their behaviour, even by a little, the public health benefit could be significant.

The high risk approach

This approach requires consideration of which population should be targeted in any prevention strategy by looking at the incidence of known risk factors and disease. As in the earlier example, information on the prevalence of risk factors and of the disease in question allows us to calculate the proportion of cases that would be prevented using different strategies. We also need to consider how and when strategies can be implemented, and whether they should take place in the community, within hospitals or primary health care.

Prevention strategies, especially those promoted by governments and medical practitioners, tend to focus on the high risk approach, targeting individuals who are known to be at an increased risk for a particular disease. The rationale for implementing a targeted approach is that it will be more cost-effective than a population approach as there is an increased likelihood that individuals who recognize they are in a high risk group will comply and therefore benefit from the intervention. Also, as we have previously discussed, the high risk individual is more likely to benefit from modifying their behaviour. A focus on the individual is perceived to be easier to promote as the impact of high risk behaviours is more apparent to those at greatest risk. Another benefit of the high risk approach is that it fits in with society's perception of the role of medical intervention and so focuses on needy individuals, rather than aiming to change the behaviour of the whole population to achieve general health gains.

Limitations of the high risk approach

The high risk approach may not be appropriate in circumstances where a small risk affects a large proportion of the population and will therefore generate a large number of cases.

The high risk approach also has other weaknesses. In assessing whether an individual is in a high risk group, the tests used have to have sufficient sensitivity and specificity (see Chapter 12) to confer an accurate diagnosis. Labelling individuals as high risk can be stigmatizing, and mislabelling can cause unnecessary anxiety in healthy individuals. Once epidemiological studies have identified risky and healthy behaviours, it could be argued that all individuals should be privy to this information and be able to improve their general health. With a high risk strategy for prevention, the positive messages of a healthier lifestyle may only reach a small proportion of the population.

Another limitation of this approach is that it does not, generally speaking, seek to change the circumstances that encourage exposure to a known risk factor, it only looks to change the exposure. The high risk approach has been described by Rose (1992) as 'palliative and temporary' as it does not address the root causes of a risky exposure. An example here would be an intervention to vaccinate people at risk of a water-borne disease without efforts to improve the quality of the local water supply.

To comply with a public health intervention, an individual may well want to know the absolute risk they have of developing a disease and by how much they are likely to reduce their risk if they modify their behaviour. Unfortunately, at an individual level, it is often very difficult to quantify the change in risk that a person might expect as a result of changing behaviour. High risk strategies can be expensive to implement and may only contribute marginally to disease control if the strategy is only able to identify a small proportion of those at risk. Information on the distribution of risk and exposure and an affordable and effective intervention are needed to ensure that high risk strategies can have a significant public health impact.

The population approach

The most important feature of the population approach to prevention is that it recognizes that considerable reductions in public health risk can be achieved by influencing change at a population rather than individual level. Where there is a clear dose–response relationship with the outcome of concern – for example, blood pressure – a shift in the whole population towards lower levels is desirable. It is important to note that knowledge of the dose–response curve is necessary, as there may be health implications for patients in the tails of the distribution.

An example would be body mass index (weight in kilograms divided by the square of height in metres), where a low value could be as harmful as a value above the accepted norm. We have discussed some of the weaknesses of the population approach in terms of difficulties motivating the overtly healthy individual at low risk, but this approach can be very beneficial in situations where there is a clear increase in risk for a given increase in the level of the exposure.

In summary, the population approach influences change towards a healthier society and recognizes the limited impact of an approach aimed at the individual.

Doctors typically classify people as being 'sick' or 'not sick', 'diseased' or 'not diseased'. This is necessary to the diagnostic and treatment process: decisions need to be made whether or not to admit a patient, whether or not to prescribe a drug, or whether or not to perform an operation. Although we often need to make decisions, this approach gives little recognition to the disease process and how it manifests in populations.

For many 'conditions', there are 'degrees of ill health'. Disease or ill health is not simply present or absent. An example is obesity: being slightly overweight can merge with being more overweight which can merge with being labelled 'obese' unless the same technical definition is used universally.

The same applies to the presence of risk factors for disease: individuals are not simply exposed or not exposed, but may be exposed to varying degrees. Furthermore, how exposure to these risk factors is distributed within the population, and how disease outcomes relate to the presence of the risk factor, will have an influence on the preventive strategy we adopt.

Rose (1992) argued that as disease and ill health come in all grades of severity the task of preventive medicine becomes more complex. It is not only the extreme cases of disease that require our attention, but also the much larger proportion of people with some features of a particular disease.

When describing the prevention paradox, we saw that a large number of people must take precautions in order to prevent illness in only a few, and that those few with very high risk factors may not benefit much themselves from participating in preventive initiatives which are directed primarily at the general population.

Some preventive measures can only be implemented on a mass scale, for example, the fluoridation of water to prevent tooth decay, legislation on environmental matters to control air pollution, and the widespread use of health education through the mass media to inform people how to avoid exposure to the HIV virus.

In contrast, certain preventive policies are directed more specifically at those at high risk of the disease in question. Attempts to increase the efficiency of services have also led to a greater degree of targeting: getting the intervention to those who are likely to show the greatest benefit. The high risk strategy implies identification of the minority that are at increased risk. How appropriate this is depends on how easy it is to identify individuals at high risk and how easy it is to differentiate them from the majority.

The shape of the dose–response curve is an important influence on strategies for prevention.

Activity 10.1

Describe each of the dose–response relationships shown in Figure 10.1 and their implications for prevention policy.

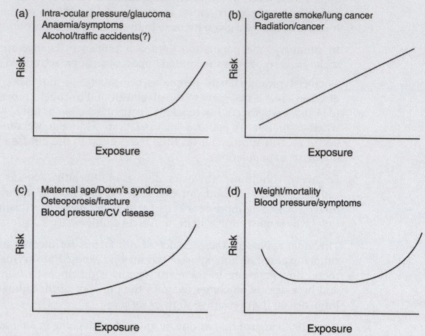

Figure 10.1 Schematic models of four possible relationships between exposure to a cause and the associated risk of disease

Source: Rose (1992)

Feedback

Your answers should be along the following lines:

1 a) Exposure increases without adverse effects until a particular level is reached. For example, an increase in intra-ocular (inside the eye) pressure is not dangerous until it exceeds certain levels; at those levels, the incidence of glaucoma (increased pressure in the eye, eventually leading to loss of sight) rises rapidly. In this case, keeping pressures below a certain level is desirable, but there is little point in being much below the danger level. At the same time, however, we must recognize that the level at which adverse effects become manifest is derived from whole populations: among individuals, some will have adverse outcomes at lower than this level and some will be well despite being above this level.

   b) This shows a linear dose–response relationship (more accurately described here as an exposure–response relationship). The greater the exposure, the greater the risk: there is even an increased risk at very low exposure levels, as with cigarette smoking and the risk of lung cancer. Even with the small amounts of tobacco smoke associated with passive smoking, there is an increased risk of lung cancer. There is no such thing as a safe exposure level. Total removal of the hazard would require an end to all exposure. Shifting people's exposures towards lower levels will invariably bring beneficial effects, so this should be the public health objective.

c) A curved relationship of exposure to risk is usually a more accurate description than the oversimplified linear exposure–response relationship. For example, the incidence of Down's syndrome increases over the whole range of maternal age, but the slope is shallow below the age of around 30 years. Thereafter, the risk of having a baby born with Down's syndrome begins to increase and it may be desirable to screen all women over this age.

d) This is more complex. It fits in with the lay view that 'moderation is good; extremes are bad'. It shows a wide band of exposures during which exposure carries no increased risk of disease. For example, for a given body size, there are a wide range of weights which carry no increased risk of disease. At the extremes of low weight and high weight, however, there may be associated disease hazards. A policy which sought to decrease body weight for the entire population might shift some people into the extreme range associated with increased levels of mortality. For this dose–response pattern there are problems inherent in shifting entire populations by too large a degree in either direction.

Another example may be alcohol and heart disease. High intakes of alcohol may have adverse effects on heart disease and other health problems (violence, road traffic accidents, etc.). Although not conclusive, there is some evidence to suggest that modest alcohol intake may have a protective effect for the risk of heart disease. It is therefore desirable to encourage people to reduce their alcohol intakes, but it is perhaps undesirable to encourage them to take no alcohol at all. The health promotion messages therefore need to be more sophisticated and complex making it more difficult to appropriately inform people and encourage healthy behaviour.

Activity 10.2

Figure 10.2 contrasts distributions of serum cholesterol in Japan and Finland. In what ways do differences in the distibution of a risk factor influence your choice of strategy?

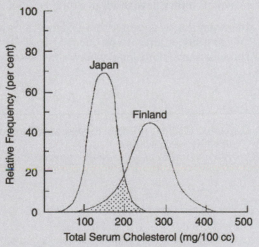

Figure 10.2 Distribution of cholesterol levels in Japan and Finland

Source: Rose (1992)

2 If one finds significant differences between populations, it suggests that some factor operating at the community level is important: there may be a genetic explanation, or differences between behaviour and/or environment of the populations (Figure 10.2). The latter two explanations would provide support for a population strategy: they suggest that the entire distribution of an exposure in a population can be shifted in a favourable (more healthy) direction if appropriate prevention policies are adopted.

There is also a suggestion that the most extreme degree of variation is in part determined by where the majority lie. This suggests, furthermore, that moderate change by the population as a whole might greatly reduce the number of people with the most conspicuous, extreme characteristics. Finally, it is possible to show that when many individuals each receive a little benefit, the total benefit to the whole population may be large.

Summary

In this chapter you have learned how information on exposures and disease can be used by individuals to improve their general health or can form part of public health strategies aimed either at those at high risk or at the general population.

A public health policy must be effective, in that it does what it purports to do, should be cost-effective and also acceptable to the population (individuals may find some invasive tests unacceptable).

In some circumstances, a preventive strategy concentrating on high risk individuals will be better than a general untargeted approach. It would, for example, not be worthwhile screening the whole population for a disease in which the incidence was low below a certain age.

In terms of acceptability however, it may be stigmatizing to focus on high risk groups. An overweight individual, for example, may feel excluded in social situations if they have to adopt a different diet.

In prevention, it is possible that a generalized message can be as potent and as valid and possibly as effective as one that concentrates on individuals. In practice, a combination of both approaches is often the most powerful.

References

Leavell HR, Clark EG (1965) *Preventative Medicine for the Doctor in His Community* (3rd edn). New York: McGraw-Hill.
Rose G (1992) *The Strategy of Preventive Medicine*. Oxford: Oxford University Press.

Epidemiological surveillance and routine data

Overview

By now you should be familiar with the principles and methods of epidemiological research. You should also be able to interpret the results of epidemiological studies and consider how they could be used to inform public health strategies. In this chapter, you will learn about public health surveillance, which describes the information systems and infrastructure used by public health agencies to monitor the health of their communities. Most countries, for example, have systems in place to monitor communicable diseases and to allow the investigation of disease outbreaks. Data collected routinely through surveillance can also be used in epidemiological research, and we will explore some of the uses of these data and their limitations.

Learning objectives

After working through this chapter you will be able to:

- **describe the purposes and methods of public health surveillance**
- **describe some types of routinely collected data**
- **discuss the advantages and limitations of data obtained from these routine sources.**

Public health surveillance

Surveillance is the examination of the occurrence and transmission of disease. You saw an early example of surveillance in Chapter 1. Through monitoring the distribution and frequency of disease and the availability of data on the population and mortality, John Snow was able to generate and test his hypotheses on drinking water as the cause of an epidemic of cholera in London in the early 1850s.

Snow used what we now term a spot map (see Figure 1.5) to plot the geographical location of all cholera deaths in an area of central London. He also determined the source of the water supply for every household in the area in order to test his hypothesis that the supply of water from the Southwark and Vauxhall water company was the source of the disease. In this way, Snow was able to use data to chart the emergence of an outbreak of disease. He was also able to ascertain the cause of the outbreak and advise on how the epidemic could be controlled.

One hundred and fifty years later, we still use the methods developed by Snow to chart the emergence of disease threats with what we term *public health surveillance*, which is defined as the systematic, continuous monitoring of the incidence and transmission of disease. Disease surveillance systems provide timely information on which to base public health interventions to control the spread of communicable diseases.

As well as local disease surveillance in various countries, the World Health Organization (WHO) coordinates a number of surveillance strategies around the world and also works to strengthen the capacity of countries to conduct effective surveillance activities. You can find out more about global communicable disease surveillance and response by visiting the WHO website: http://www.who.int/csr/labepidemiology

Purposes and methods of surveillance

Surveillance requires the systematic collection, analysis, interpretation and dissemination of health data and is essential to the planning, implementation, and evaluation of public health policies and practices. Surveillance systems can detect and verify emerging disease threats and initiate the appropriate public health response in order to minimize the impact of a disease on the health of a population.

Most countries have systems in place to monitor certain diseases (e.g. meningitis, anthrax and tuberculosis) through mandatory reporting by health care providers, including physicians, laboratories, health centres and hospitals (notifiable diseases). Risk factors for disease, such as smoking and alcohol consumption, are also monitored to review population behaviours over time.

The development of a surveillance system requires clear objectives and the use of strict criteria with which to identify and classify disease. The clear definition of a case of disease is vitally important to ensure accurate data are collected and is usually based on three criteria: clinical findings, laboratory results to confirm a diagnosis, and epidemiological data describing the time, place and type of individuals affected. A standardized way of reporting disease is very important if authorities are to have confidence in the data collected.

Surveillance systems are sometimes described as either active or passive. In *passive* surveillance, the reporting of certain diseases is automatic and routine, with an obligation on health providers, laboratories and hospitals to notify a central public health agency of all cases of a notifiable disease. *Active* surveillance is rarely carried out routinely and makes use of periodic visits to institutions to collect required data. Active surveillance may be used to monitor the spread of a new disease threat but is costly and labour-intensive. While many effective surveillance systems are in place around the world, we need to consider the fact that the proportion of notifiable disease that is reported will vary and surveillance is unlikely to capture all disease. Estimates of disease incidence in a population are therefore likely to be conservative.

Baseline data

The regular, systematic and accurate reporting of disease allows the epidemiologist to determine the usual (baseline) rates of disease incidence in a population. If disease trends are known and documented, deviations from the norm can easily be detected. A sudden increase in the incidence of measles in a population, for example, can then be investigated and reasons for this postulated, such as a reduction in the uptake of the measles, mumps and rubella (MMR) vaccine. When looking at routine data, any changes in the way data are collected or in the definition of a case of disease can affect the observed rates of disease incidence. Any alterations should be documented and considered when interpreting a change in the expected incidence of disease.

Time trends

We can now see how useful routine disease monitoring can be in detecting a sudden variation in disease incidence. Not only can it can help identify outbreaks, but it also allows us to look at variations in disease incidence over time (*time trends*). These routinely collected data sources can allow us to look at the impact of public health interventions – for example, the effect of vaccination policies or the removal of a potentially harmful exposure.

We always need to carefully consider all possible explanations for changes in disease incidence over time. Observed incidence may increase, for example, if awareness of a condition is heightened after a real, or suspected, outbreak. After an outbreak, an examining doctor may be more likely to diagnose, and so report, a particular disease and incidence will appear to increase. This bias is often described as *case-ascertainment bias*.

Patterns of disease

When looking at routine data over time, it is interesting to note any seasonal variation in the observed rates. A seasonal variation in cardiac mortality, for example, has been noted in both the northern and southern hemispheres, with higher death rates during winter than summer months (Seto *et al.* 1998; Eurogroup 1997). It has been suggested that falls in temperature may be responsible for peaks in cardiac mortality during winter months (Weerasignhe *et al.* 2002) and, interestingly, trends show that winter mortality has decreased over time with improvements in adequate heating (Seretakis *et al.* 1997). The effect of seasonality has also been shown to increase with age (Douglas *et al.* 1991). Expected seasonal variation must be incorporated into any estimates of the usual (baseline) incidence of disease, mortality or hospital admission rate.

Types of routine data

We have described public health surveillance measures that monitor the incidence of disease, help predict outbreaks and lead to the instigation of measures to control the spread of infectious pathogens. We will now discuss some of these other sources of routine data that are collected around the world, for example, mortality statistics, morbidity statistics, including data from hospitals and disease registers, and population data. As well as providing a great deal of baseline descriptive information on the health of a population, these data sources can be used by the epidemiologist to generate hypotheses on the causes of disease. The accuracy of routine data will depend on the level of infrastructure available to collect them and also on how they are used – the greater the use of a source of data, the greater the incentive to ensure that the data are complete, valid and accurate.

Demographic data

Population statistics and basic demographic data are essential to the epidemiologist. When describing and comparing the rates of disease between populations, we need to know the size of the local population to provide a denominator for estimates of prevalence and incidence. It would be meaningless to say that there are 43 cases of a disease in village A and 107 in village B without calculating and comparing the proportion of the resident populations that are afflicted by the disease in question. If we have population estimates of 1053 for village A and 3568 for village B, we can calculate the disease burden and see that the prevalence of disease is higher in village A (village A 4.1%, village B 3.0%).

The WHO publishes population estimates and core health indicators for all of its 192 member states. Although not as detailed as some locally collected data, this information is invaluable when describing the relative burden of disease around the world. Descriptive data for one country can be compared with its geographical neighbours using the WHO data available on the Internet at http://www3.who.int/whosis/country/indicators

In the United Kingdom a census of the population every 10 years provides a large amount of descriptive information, which is used extensively by both policy makers and researchers. As well as population estimates by age, sex and geographical district, there are also data on ethnicity, religion, health status and level of education. Between census surveys annual statistical projections are made to provide data for intervening years. The census is administered and analysed by the Office for National Statistics (ONS) which also carries out a multipurpose continuous survey called the General Household Survey (GHS). The GHS collects information on a range of topics from employment and education to sports and leisure, tobacco and alcohol consumption, marital status and use of health services. The survey started in 1971 and collects data annually from a sample of people living in private households in Great Britain. These data sources provide insights into health status and associated characteristics.

Since 1991, a series of surveys have been carried out each year by the Department of Health known as the Health Survey for England (HSE) which are designed to provide regular information on various aspects of the nation's health. The surveys concentrate on different demographic groups or disease conditions (and their risk factors) each year and look at health indicators such as cardiovascular disease, physical activity, eating habits, oral health, accident and asthma.

Similar surveys are carried out in the USA (e.g. the National Health and Nutrition Examination Survey) and other industrialized nations.

Mortality data

As well as population estimates, most countries collect data on date, age, sex and cause of death through official death certification. Mortality data are a well-used proxy measure for the level of disease in a population and can allow comparisons of disease-specific death rates between countries. In the UK, the ONS produces guidelines for doctors on the completion of the official Medical Certificate of Cause of Death, and has guidance on which certificate to use (stillbirth, neonatal or other death certificate), and how the cause of death should be described. Routine mortality statistics are usually based on identifying a single underlying cause for each death, and this is defined by the WHO as:

a) the disease or injury which initiated the train of events directly leading to death, or
b) the circumstances of the accident or violence which produced the fatal injury.

The underlying cause for death is the most useful data source for public health purposes, but as well as this primary cause of death, significant conditions or diseases, for example diabetes, which may have contributed to death, will also be recorded. To increase the validity of the data collected, suspicious, unexpected, or violent deaths are referred to a coroner for further investigation. So that comparisons can be made, a single standardized coding system is used when death certificates are collated. Trained personnel use the International Classification of Disease (ICD), the 10th version of which was published in 1992, to code cause of death. The WHO collates data on registered deaths by age group, sex, year and cause of death for individual member states as part of its mandate to provide health information worldwide.

Completeness of mortality statistics

'Completeness' refers to the proportion of all deaths that are registered in a population. Although developed countries report 100% completeness of death certification, in low income countries reporting of death may be poor. Completeness will be affected by the level of infrastructure in place to certify and collate data on numbers and causes of death. Rural areas are likely to have fewer medical practitioners to certify deaths, and access to health services, which collate data, may be difficult. In some parts of the world, religious, cultural or political pressures may lessen the accuracy of death certification of diseases that are deemed to be socially less acceptable. Religious or cultural beliefs may also lessen the use of necropsy to determine cause of death in suspicious or violent circumstances.

We can also consider the 'coverage' of mortality data, estimates of which are calculated by dividing the total annual deaths reported for a country by the total deaths estimated for that year for the national population. The WHO estimates coverage rates, and differences between actual and estimated deaths may be caused by the use of different population denominators – for example, the inclusion of the deaths of nationals dying abroad.

If we consider the process of registering and collating data on causes of death, we can see that there are many possible sources of error: the accuracy of the clinical diagnosis, of completion of the registration of death and of its subsequent coding all have to be considered when using and interpreting these data.

Health indices derived from mortality data and their uses

Mortality data can be used to calculate a number of health indices. Neonatal and infant deaths have been used over the years as an index of health and the provision of medical care to large populations. In the UK, infant deaths (deaths under 1 year of age) have fallen from about 150 per 1000 live births in the mid-1850s to 5.3 per 1000 in 2003. Even in relatively recent years, mortality has fallen dramatically from 18 per 1000 in 1970 to less than 6 per 1000 by the mid-1990s. This dramatic decline can be regarded as evidence of improvements in medical care, sanitation and housing. Other routinely published indices include maternal and child mortality and standardized mortality ratios which we discussed in Chapter 2.

Morbidity data

Mortality data are a very useful source of information for the researcher, but we need to know more than the causes of death in a population. What about the burden of non-fatal chronic conditions or the incidence of certain cancers? Knowledge of the disease distribution in a population can help governments plan health services and allocate medical resources more effectively, as well as allow the epidemiologist to make hypotheses on the possible determinants of disease.

Communicable diseases

We have described the importance of surveillance systems to detect outbreaks of infectious disease. Data on notifiable diseases are collected and reported by public health agencies, for example, the Centre for Disease Surveillance and Control (CDSC), a division of the Health Protection Agency, in the UK and the Centers for Disease Control and Prevention in the USA. In the UK there are 30 notifiable diseases, and doctors are required by law to inform the local authority of all suspected cases. Local authority officers are required to report all cases of disease to the CDSC every week. The CDSC then has responsibility for collating these weekly returns and publishing analyses of local and national trends. Similar systems are in place in countries around the world. Through its Department of Communicable Disease Surveillance and Response (CSR), the WHO monitors international public health and aims to strengthen the capacity of countries to conduct effective surveillance activities.

The WHO plays a vital role in monitoring global disease outbreaks and has the authority to intervene to limit the spread of disease from one country to another. In 1948 the WHO constitution was published, and in 1951 member states adopted the International Sanitary Regulations, which were renamed the International Health Regulations in 1969. These regulations were originally intended to help monitor and control six serious infectious diseases around the world: cholera, plague, yellow fever, smallpox, relapsing fever and typhus. Today, only cholera, plague and yellow fever are global notifiable diseases.

Effective systems may be in place to monitor disease outbreaks, but how confident can we be about the data they provide? Notification rates depend primarily on whether affected individuals seek medical advice. In some communities, health care providers may be difficult to access or patients may be unaware of their condition and so not seek help. As we have discussed, incidence rate estimates rely on the accurate diagnosis of disease and the information being passed to the appropriate agency.

Notification of disease is, however, only the beginning; public health agencies need the resources and infrastructure to be able to act on this information and stop the spread of the disease as quickly as possible. Health care workers may be less likely to report disease if they have little confidence those agencies will respond and effectively curb the disease.

Health centre and hospital data

Health care providers routinely collect data describing the numbers and types of patients they see and treat. These activity data can be very interesting to the researcher. Cancer diagnoses, for example, are recorded in registers to allow the monitoring of trends in cancer incidence, prevalence and survival over time and allow the epidemiologist to develop hypotheses on the possible causes of disease by looking at different local exposures. Since the 1960s, regional registries in England have collected information on all cancers diagnosed in their area. Standardized data are submitted to a central agency, the National Cancer Intelligence Centre (NCIC) at the ONS, which then coordinates collation of these data and carries out secondary analysis and research. Similar systems are in place in Scotland and Wales (see http://www.publications.doh.gov.uk/cancer/index.htm). Data from regional registries can also inform the evaluation of the effectiveness of cancer prevention and screening programmes.

Primary care or family physicians will keep data on patients' contacts and, if patients are admitted to hospital, data are collected on the length of hospital stay and the interventions, for example surgical operations, which take place. Information on some patient outcomes is also collected so that health care providers can monitor the quality of care. Both the health care provider and user want to know how long patients are likely to stay in hospital and whether their operation is expected to be a success. Knowledge of survival rates is crucial. By analysing data on outcomes from previous patients, health care providers can give patients useful information but can also plan, monitor and improve their services.

Hospital admissions for a particular condition do not, however, provide accurate estimates of the incidence of disease in a population. When interpreting data from health care providers, we need to be aware that these data may be influenced by factors other than underlying disease morbidity in a population. Patients who seek traditional therapies or medical treatments from the private or voluntary sectors will not be included in estimates of disease incidence calculated from public hospital data.

Resources to provide health care are likely to be limited, so certain criteria will have to be met before a patient is accepted for treatment. Disease severity may be a criterion, for example, and questionnaires could be used to quantify how much a condition affects a patient's life. Patients with arthritis, for example, might only be considered for joint replacement surgery after they reach a certain score on a mobility scale. Patients with benign prostate enlargement are also only considered for transurethral resection once their symptoms reach a particular level of severity.

Estimates of expected length of stay in hospital may not depend entirely on the severity of the disease in question. They may also depend on the level of support available to a patient after they have been discharged. An elderly patient, for example, may be able to leave hospital after a few days if they have the support of family while they convalesce but may have to stay in hospital for an extended period in the absence of support.

Additional sources of morbidity data

Many countries have developed registers for chronic conditions such as cancers (mentioned above), diabetes and heart disease. Disease registers can allow the monitoring of patients over time and can be used to coordinate recall of patients to attend health centres for regular check-ups and reviews of medication.

Registers are also used for surveillance. In the UK, the National Congenital Anomaly System (NCAS) was established in 1964 in response to the thalidomide tragedy. Thalodomide was licensed for use by pregnant women to combat morning sickness but it caused limb malformations in the unborn child. The NCAS was set up to detect new hazards and help prevent a similar tragedy. Although the main purpose of the NCAS is surveillance, it also provides valuable birth prevalence data for England and Wales.

Australia's Northern Territory reports the highest published incidence of acute rheumatic fever (ARF) in the world amongst its Aboriginal population. Since recurrent cases of ARF lead to cumulative heart valve damage, ARF is a significant cause of cardiovascular morbidity and mortality for these communities. Since 1997, a rheumatic heart disease control programme has established a computerized register of all known or suspected cases of ARF or rheumatic heart disease within the region. The register is used to improve patient care, particularly secondary prevention, by establishing a reminder system for monthly penicillin injections and other clinical follow-up by the primary care system and to organize and conduct education programmes.

Controlling for age and other confounders

The incidence or prevalence rates of disease can be calculated if we have the number of cases of a disease and an estimate of the size of the population in which the cases were identified. Since they do not take into account different age structures in the population, these rates are called 'crude' estimates (see Chapter 2). By looking at category-specific measures – for example, age-related incidence rates – we can look at the pattern of disease in a population, to help us to target public health interventions. Although crude rates of disease can be a useful summary, comparing crude measures between populations can be misleading if these populations differ with respect to underlying characteristics, such as age or sex. Controlling for confounding factors such as age and sex through indirect standardization was dealt with in Chapter 2.

Variation in available data

As we have discussed, the type and quality of routine data in terms of completeness and validity depend primarily on available resources. Some low income countries may only have the funds and infrastructure to collect high level data on disease incidence and death. Those countries with multicultural and multinational populations also find it useful to look at health-related data on ethnicity to investigate any variation in diagnoses and use of services. Data can also be compared across regions and can be linked to deprivation scores. Data on socioeconomic status are often collected and so inequalities in health and the use of health care can also be investigated.

In other countries, data on additional descriptive variables may be needed to investigate the burden of disease in a community and look at the patterns and potential reasons for high disease incidences or use of health services.

Value of routine data

We have discussed some of the sources of routine data and how they might be used by a researcher. We have also outlined some of the difficulties in interpreting analyses of routine data. The most valuable attribute of these data, however, is that they are generally available at little or no cost. They supply us with baseline information to describe a population, and variations in health outcome by age, sex, ethnicity or geography, for example, can instigate investigations into underlying causes of disease. If routine data are collected systematically over time, we have access to information on the progression of a disease in a population or the impact of a health intervention such as screening or vaccination. We can link data sets to consider the effects of confounding and use these data to generate hypotheses on the determinants of disease. Data linkage can be used to follow up an occupational cohort (e.g. miners or asbestos workers) and detect new cases of a certain disease, admission to hospital or death. Standardized mortality ratios allow us to compare mortality between populations and may suggest the need to look for an environmental determinant or local exposure. Data on migrant studies can be used in the same way, and data over time can demonstrate changes in significant exposures as migrant populations adopt the characteristics of their host populations.

Ecological studies

We can use routine population-based data to generate hypotheses in what are known as ecological studies (see Chapter 5 for more details). Ecological studies use routine data to relate the frequency of an exposure to an outcome of interest. A study in South America, for example, used data from a national survey of breast-feeding to compare the prevalence of breast-feeding with data on infant mortality (Betrán *et al.* 2001). The authors found higher rates of deaths from diarrhoeal disease and acute respiratory infections in babies that were not breast-fed. Another study in Sweden used available data to analyse trends in rates of chlamydia infection and ectopic pregnancy (Egger *et al.* 1998) and found that in women aged 20–24 years there was a strong correlation between the rate of ectopic pregnancy and the rate of chlamydial infection in the same year. This type of study is known as a cross-sectional ecological study, is quick and easy to perform and can generate hypotheses as to the possible aetiology of disease.

Ecological studies can also be longitudinal and look at trends in a defined population over time. Birth cohorts have been the subject of many ecological studies and explore disease trends in a group of individuals born in a certain time period. A number of studies have looked at poverty and inequality data, related them to mortality statistics and demonstrated strong positive correlation between socio-economic status and mortality.

A recent ecological study by Whitley *et al.* (1999) used routine data to investigate the association between death from suicide and indices of social deprivation and fragmentation. Although geographical studies have shown suicide rates to be linked to deprivation, this study included data on the underlying social character-istics of a population. Census data on private renting, single households and mari-tal status as well as data on mean abstention rates from voting and deprivation scores were correlated with suicide rates in 633 Parliamentary consistuencies in Great Britain. Suicide rates were found to be more strongly associated with these measures of social fragmentation than with poverty.

Although these ecological studies can provide us with very interesting correlations between exposures and disease, we cannot draw any causal conclusions from these analyses. The unit of analysis in these studies is a population, not an individual, and we do not know whether the individuals exposed are the same as those who develop the disease. In the Egger *et al.* study, for example, we do not know whether the women who had confirmed chlamydial infection where the same women who went on to have ectopic pregnancies.

Another potential misinterpretation of findings from an ecological study is described as the ecological fallacy: a study may demonstrate that two variables are positively correlated, but this cannot be interpreted to indicate that all individuals susceptible to a particular exposure will go on to develop the disease in question. Looking at data from the Whitley study, we cannot infer that all socially fragmented individuals will die prematurely from suicide.

Limitations of routine data

Although routine data can be very useful, the ways in which they were collected and their primary purpose need to be understood if they are to be correctly inter-preted. Data collected as part of a research study will be less prone to biases and the effects of missing information. In some cases, but not all, researchers are trained in the methods of data collection and use strict inclusion and exclusion criteria when admitting individuals to a study. Routinely collected data, on the other hand, may be collected by a large number of people, with little training, across many sites. The comparability of collected data may therefore be compromised. Whether data are fed back to the individuals involved in collecting them may also influence their quality, as the motivation to ensure data are of a high standard will increase. As we have mentioned, when collecting data on the incidence of disease, the capacity and infrastructure to elicit the appropriate public health response may affect the commitment to ensuring data are collected systematically. Some benefits and limitations of routine data can be seen in Table 11.1.

Table 11.1 How useful are routinely collected data?

Benefits of routine data	Limitations of routine data
Good availability	Often incomplete and inaccurate
Usually inexpensive	Prone to bias
Timely	Limited descriptive variables (e.g. socioeconomic status or ethnicity)
Allow development of hypotheses	Often poorly presented or analysed
Provide baseline data	May be subject to manipulation
	Non-standardized definitions used

Enhancing the value of routine data

We are aware of the limitations of some sources of routine data but we can still make good use of them. Where the completeness of data is considered poor, knowledge of the types of people for whom data are not available is valuable when determining the direction of potential biases. For example, we can consider that mortality statistics for some infectious diseases may be underreported and so estimates are likely to be conservative. Use of, or access to, health services may be affected by socioeconomic status or ethnicity and so, with knowledge of determinants of health, we can make inferences about related data sources.

The use of electronic methods to collect and collate data will improve accuracy and allow more complex analyses. Data can then be used more widely. The importance of collecting high quality data is strengthened as the use of data grows and more agencies, including policy makers and the media, have access to descriptive information on the health of populations.

Going beyond routine data

While descriptive information on the health and well-being of a population is sometimes not routinely available, you learned earlier in this book about a number of research methods that can be used to collect it. Of course, primary data collection will usually incur a cost. Look back at Chapters 4–8 to remind yourself of the advantages and disadvantages of the different types of epidemiological studies and surveys.

Have a go at the following two activities that will help you to consolidate some of the things you have learned.

 Activity 11.1

Zimbabwe has a population of about 13 million (2002) of whom nearly 40% live in areas affected by malaria. Although a malaria control programme has been in operation since 1948, malaria continues to be one of the common causes of morbidity and mortality in Zimbabwe, causing up to 20% of childhood deaths in some areas of the country. In 1996 the Ministry of Health reviewed the data from routine surveillance systems in order to assess the burden of malaria in the country and to introduce additional control measures. The data obtained in this review are used here to highlight the benefits and limitations of data from routine surveillance systems.

The numbers of clinical malaria cases and deaths from malaria reported each year between 1997 and 2002 by all government health facilities are shown in Figure 11.1.

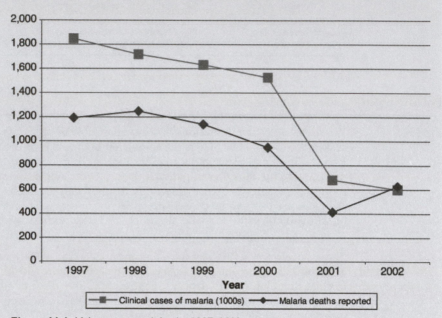

Figure 11.1 Malaria cases and deaths, 1997–2002

Source: based on data from the WHO regional office for Africa (www.afro.who.int/malaria/)

1 Describe what these data tell us about malaria and malaria deaths in Zimbabwe.

2 What are the limitations of these data?

3 What further information would you need to assess the burden of malaria?

 Feedback

Your answers should be along the following lines.

1 There was a small steady decline of 15.8% in the number of cases of malaria between 1997 and 2000. A large drop in cases of 55% was observed from 2000 to 2001. After this, the rate of decline fell back down to a conservative decrease of 12%.

With the exception of a small rise in the number of malarial deaths from 1997 to 1998, the rate of deaths from malaria largely mirrored the number of reported cases until 2001. As with reported cases, the rate of decrease was highest between 2000 and 2001 after which a slight increase was seen.

It is unclear why a rise in the number of deaths has been seen from 2001 to 2002.

2 These data are limited by selection bias and measurement bias:

Selection bias. These data are from a selected group of people who attend government health facilities. Since there are several other sources of health care (e.g. private and traditional practitioners), these data are unlikely to reflect the total burden of malaria in Zimbabwe.

Measurement bias. The accuracy, consistency and completeness of such data are debatable since they are collected from several institutions involving different categories of health workers over long periods. Any changes to collection systems will also affect the comparability of data.

3 There are three further types of information you need in order to assess the burden of malaria in the country.

Data on population. Since the population at risk is not given, it is not possible to estimate the annual incidence of malaria and thus the magnitude of the burden of malaria cannot be clearly assessed.

Age and sex distribution of cases and deaths. This information is important in assessing the magnitude of the burden of malaria because, generally speaking, malaria mortality is higher in children under 5 years old than in adults.

Frequency distribution of other causes of morbidity and mortality. This information is needed to assess the relative public health importance of malaria.

Activity 11.2

In this activity, you will need to consider the strengths and limitations of routine data in comparison to data obtained from epidemiological studies such as cross-sectional surveys.

You are responsible for a new government initiative to assess the risks posed to men and women in the workplace. You have been given a limited budget and time period to collect data and write your report. After some preliminary fact-finding, you consider whether to conduct a cross-sectional survey of the working population or to review the available data from routine surveillance systems.

1 What are the strengths and limitations of these two options?

2 Which method will you decide to use? Support your answer with reasons.

Feedback

1 Table 11.2 lists the strengths and weaknesses of the two approaches. Although the issues mentioned focus on injuries, most of them are generally applicable to measuring the burden of disease and other health conditions.

2 As the programme manager responsible for collecting baseline information on injuries, you would most likely recommend an initial review of the data already available from the passive surveillance system and an assessment of the quality of those data

considering all the potential sources of bias. Most probably, the available data would not be adequate to establish accurately the burden of disease due to injury, the spectrum of injury or the factors associated with injury. If that were the case, you could suggest a baseline survey to supplement the surveillance systems so as to gain a better understanding of the burden of injury and to identify appropriate control measures.

Table 11.2 Strengths and limitations of surveys and passive surveillance systems

Characteristic	Survey	Routine surveillance system
Prevalence and incidence	The prevalence of different types of injury can be measured	The incidence of injury can be measured, but the quality of data depends on several factors such as characteristics of reporting centres, data collection tools and system, the health care-seeking behaviour of the population
Spectrum of injury	The spectrum of injury including those that do not warrant medical care can be established	Only data on individuals who reported their injury will be collected
Factors associated with injury	In-depth data on several factors associated with injury can be obtained	Data on factors associated with injury are limited
Accuracy of data	Since it is feasible to control the quality of data, the prevalence and spectrum of injury can be estimated more accurately	Estimates of incidence of injury might not be accurate since it is often difficult to link the number of cases of injury to the actual population at risk
Relation of data	The data represent one point in time, so they have limited value for the analysis of trends over time	Since the data would be available for a longer period, trends can be monitored over time
Feasibility and cost of study	Although highly feasible, this can be expensive since it involves development of data collection tools, training and supervision of personnel, and transport and subsistence	Review of data from surveillance systems is relatively cheap, especially if the data are compiled and analysed regularly

Summary

You should now understand that although there are several limitations to interpreting data from routine sources, they do give valuable information. Since these data are collected by most public health agencies, they are a relatively cheap way to establish baseline data. This information can also allow us to identify disease outbreaks and epidemics, monitor time trends and seasonal patterns, evaluate disease interventions and generate hypotheses as to the possible causes of disease.

You should be able to describe the purposes and methods of public health surveillance.

You should also be able to discuss the advantages and limitations of data obtained from routine sources.

References

Betrán AP, de Onís M, Lauer JA *et al.* (2001) Ecological study of effect of breast feeding on infant mortality in Latin America. *British Medical Journal* 323: 303.

Douglas AS, Allan TM, Rawles JM (1991) Composition of seasonality of disease. *Scottish Medical Journal* 36: 76–82.

Egger M, Low N, Davey Smith G *et al.* (1998) Screening for chlamydial infections and the risk of ectopic pregnancy in a county in Sweden: ecological analysis. *British Medical Journal* 316: 1776–80.

Eurowinter Group (1997) Cold exposure and winter mortality from ischaemic heart disease, cerebrovascular disease, respiratory disease, and all causes, in warm and cold regions of Europe. *Lancet* 349: 1341–6.

Seretakis D, Lagiou P, Lipworth L *et al.* (1997) Changing seasonality of mortality from coronary heart disease. *Journal of the American Medical Association* 278: 1012–14.

Seto TB, Mittleman MA, Davis RB *et al.* (1998) Seasonal variation in coronary artery disease mortality in Hawaii: observational study. *British Medical Journal* 316: 1946–7.

Weerasinghe DP, MacIntyre CR, Rubin GL (2002) Seasonality of coronary deaths in New South Wales, Australia. *Heart* 88(1): 30–4.

Whitley E, Gunnell D, Dorling D *et al.* (1999) Ecological study of social fragmentation, poverty, and suicide. *British Medical Journal* 319: 1034–7.

12 Screening and diagnostic tests

Overview

The previous chapters have focused on the principles and methods of epidemiological study and gaining knowledge of the distribution and determinants of disease. In this chapter we look at the value of a type of secondary prevention called screening. Screening is a way of improving patient outcomes by detecting a disease at an earlier, more treatable stage, or by avoiding recurrence of disease.

In order to provide effective curative or preventive health care, it is necessary to distinguish between individuals who have a disease and those who do not. For this purpose, there are tests such as physical examination; biochemical assay of blood, urine and other body fluids; radiography; ultrasonography; cytology; and histopathology. One question we need to answer is how good these tests are at separating individuals with and without the disease in question. Unfortunately, several screening and diagnostic tests are liable to error. In this chapter, you will learn about certain statistical methods for assessing the quality of screening and diagnostic tests to help you make informed decisions about their use and interpretation.

Learning objectives

After working through this chapter, you will be better able to:

- **describe and calculate the measures of validity of a diagnostic test**
- **explain the relationship between prevalence and predictive values**
- **list the World Health Organization guidelines for assessing appropriateness of screening**
- **describe and calculate the measure of reliability of a test.**

Definition and purpose of screening

The aim of screening is to identify asymptomatic disease, or risk factors for disease, by testing a population that has not yet developed clinical symptoms. Screening tests are often not diagnostic and usually seek to identify small numbers of individuals at high risk of a particular condition. Further tests are needed to confirm a diagnosis. Efficacious screening rests on the premise that the detection of early disease, and subsequent effective treatment, will beneficially alter the natural course of the disease and thus improve patient outcomes.

Screening is usually considered as an example of secondary prevention (see Chapter 10), although primary prevention screening can be used to identify patients with an exposure to a risk factor, instead of a disease. For example, screening individuals for high blood cholesterol levels seeks to identify those at higher risk of coronary heart disease for targeted health promotion or cholesterol-lowering drug treatment. Screening is also used for other purposes such as selection of people fit enough for a job or containment of infection (e.g. screening new nurses or teachers for tuberculosis or food handlers for salmonella).

Screening is not universally beneficial and the course of certain diseases may not be altered through early identification especially if, for example, there is no available and effective treatment. Screening programmes need to be properly evaluated before they are implemented, using the methods already described in this book. The ethics of screening also needs to be considered; this and other criteria for screening are discussed later in this chapter.

Mass or targeted screening

A screening programme can either include the whole population (*mass* screening) or selected groups who are anticipated to have an increased prevalence of the condition for which screening has been instituted (*targeted* screening). An example of mass screening would be to measure the blood pressure of all adults in a population. Measuring blood cholesterol in relatives of people with familial hyperlipidaemia is an example of targeted screening.

Reliability and validity of a screening test

An effective screening programme will use a test that is able to differentiate between individuals with a disease, or its precursor, and those without. This property of a test is known as its *validity*. A screening test should also ideally be inexpensive, easy to administer and impose minimal discomfort on those to whom it is administered. It also needs to be *reliable* in that it measures a variable consistently and is free of random error.

A clinical test has yet to be developed that is able to determine with 100% accuracy all those with and without a particular sign or symptom. A measure of a screening test's *sensitivity* is the proportion of 'true positives' correctly identified with a subsequent diagnostic test. If sensitivity is low, it suggests that a number of positive cases have been missed. These are termed the 'false negatives'. A false positive screening test can be costly for both the service provider and the patient. A measure of a test's *specificity* is the proportion of 'true negatives' correctly identified. We cannot expect sensitivity and specificity values to be equally high for a given test, and the importance of each measure will depend on the disease in question. In the case of a communicable disease, for example, sensitivity may be considered more important as a false positive case may have less of a public health impact than a false negative which could result in continued transmission of the disease.

Estimation of sensitivity and specificity will depend on the definition that is used for a true positive. This may be relatively easy when the test is for a dichotomous variable where a disease is considered to be either present or absent. For a continuous variable, such as blood pressure, the definition of a positive case needs to be determined and be evidence-based; this may be by carrying out a further 'gold standard' diagnostic test, or by following up participants to see who develops clinical manifestations of disease.

Predictive values

Another important measure for a screening test is the *predictive value*. The positive predictive value of mammography, for example, will tell a woman how likely it is that she has breast cancer after a positive mammogram. The negative predictive value will tell a woman the probability is that she truly does not have breast cancer if the mammogram is negative. Predictive values measure whether or not the individual actually has the disease, given the results of the screening test, and are determined by the validity of a test (specificity and sensitivity) and the characteristics of the population being tested (particularly the prevalence of preclinical disease).

The more sensitive a test, the less likely it is that an individual with a negative result will have the disease, so the greater the negative predictive value. The more specific a test, the less likely an individual with a positive test will be free from disease and the greater the positive predictive value. However, if the disease is rare, and the population is at a low risk of disease, the positive results are likely to be mostly false positives.

Table 12.1 summarizes the relationship between the results of a screening test and the actual presence of disease as determined by the result of a subsequent confirmatory diagnostic test (the 'gold standard'). In the table, *a* is the number of subjects who *have* the condition and are found *positive* by the test (true positives), *b* the number of subjects who *do not have* the condition but are found *positive* by the test (false positives), *c* the number of subjects who *have* the condition but are found *negative* by the test (false negatives) and *d* the number of subjects who *do not have* the condition and are found *negative* by the test (true negatives).

Table 12.1 Measuring the effectiveness of a screening test

		True disease status	
		Positive	Negative
Result of test	Positive	a	b
	Negative	c	d

$$\text{Sensitivity} = \frac{a}{a+c} \qquad\qquad \text{Positive Predictive Value} = \frac{a}{a+b}$$

$$\text{Specificity} = \frac{d}{b+d} \qquad\qquad \text{Negative Predictive Value} = \frac{d}{c+d}$$

Ethics of screening

When a patient decides to visit their family doctor, or an allied health professional, they are usually experiencing a symptom of a disease. They are willing to undergo a medical examination in the hope of elucidating the cause of their complaint, which will result in a diagnosis and, where available, a course of treatment. A screening test is an intervention that is carried out on overtly healthy individuals that have no symptoms of disease and have not initiated the request for the test. It is imperative that the potential benefits of taking part in a screening programme will outweigh the risk of harm (Cochrane and Holland 1971). Before the initiation of a screening policy, there needs to be conclusive evidence that the screening test is able to differentiate between those with and those without disease and that the available treatment will beneficially alter the natural course of the disease.

There is an ethical responsibility to make sure that individuals have enough information to make an informed decision as to whether to take part in a screening programme and that they have considered the potential benefit and harm of taking part. The ethics of screening for disease is complicated and potential policies need very careful consideration before they are made available to the public.

The risks of taking part in a screening programme can be considered for both the individual and society. While many medical tests are straightforward and present no risk, other tests may have the potential to harm the participant. Repeated exposure to X-ray radiation in mammography for breast cancer may pose a risk to the patient and the risk of miscarriage following an amniocentesis test must be explained to a pregnant woman considering testing for Down's syndrome. For some screening tests, there may also be risk attached to further confirmatory tests. Not only must any potential risks be explained to the participant, but also the fact that tests are not always able to differentiate with 100% accuracy those with and those without the disease. Even with full compliance, no screening programme will be able to detect all the cases of disease in a population (false negatives) and all screening programmes are likely to wrongly classify some patients as being diseased (false positives). A false positive test may cause unnecessary anxiety and a false negative test may result in a loss of confidence in medical intervention as well as a potential loss of life. An individual with a false negative test may later fail to recognize subsequent warning signs of the disease, which could result in a poorer prognosis on diagnosis. There may be other unwanted and unplanned effects of a positive test – for example, life insurance premiums may be increased. Even with an effective treatment, a true positive test may increase anxiety and pose a risk to mental health or quality of life.

Before the introduction of a national screening policy, the costs of the resources needed to carry out the screening tests have to be considered. Specialist equipment may be required, but also the need for appropriate staff to carry out tests and to ensure patients are appropriately counselled before and after the test will increase costs. The expected incidence of the disease, or its precursor, needs to be known to allow policy makers to anticipate the numbers of patients that are likely to need expensive treatment options. It would be unethical to screen women for breast cancer if there were insufficient numbers of doctors and nurses and hospital facilities to offer timely treatments for those found to have positive screening results.

Policy makers also need to ensure there is good quality control of the screening programme and that there is no variation in the standards and criteria used for further intervention. If these high standards are not maintained, the ethics of screening could be challenged and compliance with a programme could fall, lowering the proportion of the population likely to benefit.

Criteria for screening

We have discussed some of the potential advantages and disadvantages of participation in a screening programme both for the individual and for society. To ensure that the potential for harm is minimized, programmes need to fulfil a number of criteria that should be considered before implementation. The World Health Organization criteria for assessing the appropriateness of screening, first published by Wilson and Jungner (1968), are listed in Table 12.2.

Table 12.2 Wilson and Jungner criteria for screening (1968)

The condition being screened for should be an important health problem
The natural history should be well understood
There should be a detectable early stage
There should be a suitable test for the early stage
The test should be acceptable
Treatment at an early stage should be of more benefit than at a later stage
Intervals for repeating the test should be determined
There should be adequate health service provision for the extra clinical workload resulting from the screen
The risks, both physical and psychological, should be less than the benefits
The costs should be balanced against benefits

Source: Wilson and Jungner (1968)

Although the fundamental aspects of subsequent criteria are the same as those published by Wilson and Jungner, a number of simplifications have been. In 1984, Cuckle and Wald's (1984) simpler list of criteria is summarized in Table 12.3.

Table 12.3 Cuckle and Wald criteria for screening (1984)

Aspect	Requirement
Disorder	Well defined
Prevalence	High
Natural history	Medically important disorder for which there is an effective remedy available
Financial	Cost-effective
Facilities	Available or easily installed
Ethical	Procedure following a positive result generally agreed and acceptable
Test	Simple and safe
Test performance	Values in affected and unaffected individuals known, overlap sufficiently small and suitable cut-off level defined

Source: Cuckle and Wald (1984)

Some of these criteria are essential when considering the implementation of a screening programme. The availability of a treatment for the identified disease is essential as there would be no value in identifying diseases for which there are no effective treatments. Other criteria are more relative. For example, if a disease is very rare but very serious and easily preventable, it may still be beneficial to screen for it. Phenylketonuria, a congenitally acquired inability to metabolize the amino acid phenylalanine, is such a rare disease. If undetected, it leads to serious mental retardation. A highly sensitive and specific screening test, performed on a blood sample taken from a prick in the heel of a newborn, can identify babies who have this condition. A diet low in phenylalanine effectively prevents the development of mental retardation in such children.

Evaluating screening programmes

Once criteria for a potential screening programme have been reviewed, determining whether a particular screening programme is of value in a community will depend on the following: the relative burden of the disease; the feasibility of organizing a screening programme; the effectiveness of the programme in reducing the burden of the disease; and the cost of the programme in relation to the resources available.

Relative burden of disease

The disease in question needs to be serious and pose a significant burden to the population and to health services. Morbidity and mortality rates can help identify potential diseases for screening, but the appropriateness of the disease for screening inevitably depends on the availability of a test to detect it, an effective treatment and its relative value in comparison with other health problems.

Feasibility

Screening programmes require huge infrastructures to be in place if they are to run effectively. The feasibility of a programme will depend on a number of factors. First, the groups identified for screening have to be identified, contacted and invited to attend a programme at the appropriate time. Most screening programmes in industialized nations rely on family doctors in the community to provide information on the age, sex and medical history of the population. Electronic systems are then used to invite the population to attend for screening in a systematic manner and results are fed back to the individuals' family doctor. Compliance with a screening programme will affect feasibility. If screening tests are not considered acceptable to the population, they are less likely to attend. A dental check-up for caries every 6 months is deemed acceptable to most people, but an invasive test such as a sigmoidoscopy or colonoscopy to detect colorectal cancer may be considered much less acceptable. Unless a large proportion of those at risk attend a screening programme, it is unlikely that the burden of the disease will be reduced in the population.

As we have mentioned previously, estimates of the anticipated incidence of disease in a population will allow health services to assess whether sufficient facilities are in place to carry out diagnostic tests on those who are found positive at screening and to treat those confirmed as positive. Policy makers need to consider, for example, the affordability of providing cholesterol-lowering drugs to everyone found to have an elevated serum cholesterol level.

Effectiveness

In epidemiology the term 'effectiveness' describes the ability of an intervention to do what it purports to do. In the case of screening, the aim of a programme is to reduce the burden of a disease in a population by reducing the number of individuals that succumb to it and by offering a better prognosis to those that do. The effectiveness of a screening programme is therefore evaluated by the extent to which it can affect subsequent outcomes of disease. This is difficult to measure because of a number of biases, which affect most of the study designs used. These biases are selection bias, lead-time bias and length-time bias, and need to be considered when interpreting the results of a screening programme.

Selection bias

People who choose to participate in screening programmes often differ from those who do not. Selection bias can work both ways. People who are at high risk may be more likely to attend – for example, women with a family history of breast cancer. In some screening programmes it has been observed that individuals at lower risk are more likely to attend – for example, women at low risk of cervix cancer are more likely to accept an invitation for a smear test. Differences in morbidity or mortality between individuals who do or do not attend screening may be due in part to differences between the subjects rather than the effect of the screening programme.

Lead-time bias

If screening identifies early disease before it presents clinically, it may appear to improve survival by increasing the interval between diagnosis and death. In this way, individuals may appear to live longer. In Figure 12.1 we can see that the screening programme that led to a positive test appears to have increased survival time to 10 years (from age 55 to age 65). As screening has not delayed death, it is not beneficial and has just increased the period of time the individual was aware of his/her condition by 5 years.

Figure 12.1 Illustration of lead-time bias

	⇓	⇓	⇓
	Positive screening test	Clinical symptoms present	Death
	<-->		
	Lead time		
Age:	55 yrs	60 yrs	65 yrs

Length-time bias

A screening programme is more likely to detect a larger proportion of cases of a slowly progressive, less aggressive condition. It is also more likely to miss cases, which progress quickly and have a less favourable prognosis. Slow-growing, less aggressive conditions will invariably be present in the population for longer periods of time, and a screening programme is more likely to be successful in detecting them. For example, some breast tumours are slower-growing and spend longer in a preclinical phase. This means they are more likely to be detected at that stage and may also have a more favourable prognosis. Length-time bias might lead to a false conclusion that screening has lengthened the lives of those who were found positive. In cancer screening, for example, policy makers also need to consider how often to invite individuals for screening. The appropriate length of time between screens depends on the natural history of the disease, such as the length of the detectable preclinical stage and the treatment available at that stage.

Cost

The cost of screening programmes is an important consideration. However wealthy a society, there will always be a finite amount of resources available for health care, so the relative cost-effectiveness of a screening programme compared with other forms of health care has to be considered. These decisions are very difficult to make and have been made in the past as a result of enthusiasm for a particular screening test, without proper consideration of the effectiveness of the programmes and the related costs. Costs to be considered will be those relating to the conduct of the screening programme, the further diagnostic tests required for those labelled positive by the screening programme, and the cost of treating those in whom the disease is confirmed. On the other hand, in the absence of screening and prevention or early treatment of disease, costs will be incurred by the treatment of patients who present clinically with more advanced stages of disease.

Study designs for evaluating screening

We have considered three very powerful biases that will affect the evaluation of any screening programme and can serve to overestimate its effect on reducing the morbidity and mortality associated with a particular disease. Before a potential screening method is rolled out nationally, it needs to be properly evaluated so the expected benefits are clear. A number of study designs can be used, but most are liable to biases (see Table 12.4).

Randomized controlled trials (RCTs) are the best method for evaluating screening and are considered the gold standard for establishing the effectiveness of a policy. In RCTs, individuals will be randomly allocated to one of two groups: the screening or control group (see Chapter 8). Although some individuals will not wish to take part or will be lost to follow-up, if the proportions of patients that comply with the study protocol are the same in both groups, we can be confident that selection bias has been removed. Lead-time and length-time biases are removed when comparing the overall mortality in the two randomized groups, but adjustments for lead time and length time still need to be made when comparing the length of survival.

Table 12.4 Potential biases when evaluating screening

Study type	Method	Potential biases
Cohort	Comparing length of survival in screen-detected and non-screen-detected cases	Lead-time bias Length-time bias
Case control	Comparing screening history of cases with age-matched controls	Selection bias Assessment bias
Non-randomized trial	Comparing mortality using historical controls	Selection bias

However, when evidence of benefit has been strong, screening programmes have been implemented without supporting evidence from RCTs. Cervical cancer is a case in point: knowledge of the natural history of the disease led to the introduction of screening programmes in the UK and other industrialized nations before results from a pilot trial were available. In Iceland, Finland, Sweden and parts of Denmark, nearly complete coverage of the target population by organized cervical screening programmes was soon followed by sharp falls in incidence and mortality (Hakama and Louhivuori 1988; Sigurdsson 1993). Similar data have been published on the UK (Quinn *et al.* 1999).

Randomized trials may be the gold standard when evaluating screening, but there are a number of potential drawbacks. They are time-consuming due to the long periods of follow-up required to show differences in outcome. If a randomized trial is in progress in an area over a long period of time, it will also be prone to contamination of the control group. An awareness of the screening programme may lead subjects in the control (non-screened) group to seek out screening. Deaths in the screened group may also be more likely to be attributed to the disease under investigation, as the registering doctors' awareness of the condition may be increased. Due to the large numbers of patients required to demonstrate the effectiveness of a programme, and the length of follow-up, RCTs are expensive to carry out. Large numbers of subjects are also required where the trial is designed to show smaller benefits. If a screening test is available to patients who become aware of the ongoing RCT, despite the lack of experimental evidence as to the benefit of screening, it is sometimes difficult to justify randomizing some subjects to the non-screening arm of a trial and so alternative study designs may yield more acceptable results.

To help you consolidate what you have learned, there are a number of questions you can practice in the activity below. There is feedback after each question, but you should attempt each task before reading the feedback to it.

✐ Activity 12.1

In a hypothetical study, 1000 patients attending a hospital general outpatient department were tested for diabetes using the following two tests:

- fasting blood sugar (FBS)
- glucose tolerance test (GTT).

There were 100 patients who had a positive GTT, and they were classified as true cases of diabetes. There were also 140 patients with an FBS of at least 6 mmol/l (the cut-off point to distinguish people with diabetes from those who do not have diabetes). Among these 140 patients, only 98 were true cases of diabetes (i.e. only 98 had a positive GTT as well).

1   What are the sensitivity, specificity, and positive and negative predictive values of the FBS test in this study population?

When the cut-off point for the FBS was raised to 7 mmol/l, the sensitivity of the test decreased to 95% and the specificity increased to 98% in the hypothetical study population.

2   Calculate the positive predictive value and false negative error rate of FBS at this cut-off point.

The FBS test and GTT were used in a hypothetical community survey to screen for diabetes. Among 1000 people surveyed, 40 people had a positive GTT for diabetes and were classified as true cases of diabetes. An FBS cut-off value of 6 mmol/l was used to distinguish between people with and without diabetes; you can assume that at this cut-off point the FBS had a sensitivity of 98% and specificity of 95%.

3   What are the positive predictive value and false negative error rate of FBS in this survey?

4   Why is the positive predictive value different from that observed in the hypothetical hospital-based study?

Assume that if the cut-off point of FBS is increased to 7.5 mmol/l, the sensitivity is 90% and the specificity is 99% for diagnosing diabetes.

5   What are the positive predictive value and the false negative error rate of FBS if the cut-off point of 7.5 mmol/l is used to screen for diabetes in this community?

6   If you were asked to fix the cut-off point of FBS for a survey of your community would you select 6 mmol/l or 7 mmol/l? Give reasons for your answer.

Feedback

1   First, set up a 2 × 2 table of diabetes by true cases against FBS test results, as shown in Table 12.5. Then you can calculate the required values:

Table 12.5 Diabetes by true cases against FBS test results (cut-off 6 mmol/l)

Test results (FBS)	Diabetes (GTT)		Total
	Positive	Negative	
Positive	98	42	140
Negative	2	858	860
Total	100	900	1000

$$\text{FBS sensitivity} = \frac{98}{100} \times 100 = 98\%.$$

$$\text{FBS specificity} = \frac{858}{900} \times 100 = 95\%.$$

$$\text{FBS positive predictive value} = \frac{98}{140} \times 100 = 70\%.$$

$$\text{FBS negative predictive value} = \frac{858}{860} \times 100 = 99.8\%.$$

2 Again, you should first set up a 2 × 2 table of diabetes by true cases against test results, as shown in Table 12.6. Then you can calculate the required values:

Table 12.6 Diabetes by true cases against FBS test results (cut-off 7 mmol/l)

Test results (FBS)	Diabetes (GTT)		Total
	Positive	Negative	
Positive	95	18	113
Negative	5	882	887
Total	100	900	1000

$$\text{FBS positive predictive value} = \frac{95}{113} \times 100 = 84\%.$$

$$\text{FBS false negative error rate} = \frac{5}{100} \times 100 = 5\%.$$

Alternatively,

FBS false negative error rate = 1 − sensitivity = 1 − 95% = 5%.

3 As before, start by first setting up a 2 × 2 table of diabetes by true cases against test results, as shown in Table 12.7. Then you can calculate the required values:

Table 12.7 Diabetes by true cases against FBS test results (cut-off 6 mmol/l)

Test results (FBS)	Diabetes (GTT)		Total
	Positive	Negative	
Positive	39	48	87
Negative	1	912	913
Total	40	960	1000

$$\text{FBS positive predictive value} = \frac{39}{87} \times 100 = 45\%.$$

$$\text{FBS false negative error rate} = \frac{1}{40} \times 100 = 2.5\%.$$

4 Although the sensitivity and specificity of the FBS at this cut-off point were the same in the hypothetical hospital-based study and in the community survey, there is marked reduction in the positive predictive value of FBS in the community survey. This is due to the fact that the prevalence of diabetes in the hospital population was higher (10%) than in the community (4%).

5 Again, first set up a 2×2 table of diabetes by true cases against test results, as shown in Table 12.8. Then you can calculate the required values:

Table 12.8 Diabetes by true cases against FBS test results (cut-off 7.5 mmol/l)

Test results (FBS)	Diabetes (GTT)		Total
	Positive	Negative	
Positive	36	10	46
Negative	4	950	954
Total	40	960	1000

$$\text{FBS positive predictive value} = \frac{36}{46} \times 100 = 78\%.$$

$$\text{FBS false negative error rate} = \frac{4}{40} \times 100 = 10\%.$$

6 You would probably want to recommend 6 mmol/l as an appropriate cut-off point for FBS because the false negative error rate is lower (2.5%) at 6 mmol/l level than at 7 mmol/l. A lower false negative error rate (rather than a lower false positive error rate) can be seen as preferable for the following reasons:

a) The physical and psychological stress following a false positive test is minimal since further diagnostic tests are available to confirm or refute the diagnosis of diabetes.
b) There are effective treatments for diabetes which can prevent the later complications of untreated diabetes.

Activity 12.2

Now it is time for you to explore some of the current challenges in the implementation of screening policies. Use the Internet or go to a scientific library to look for published evidence on screening for colorectal cancer. Use this information to explore reasons for and against screening. Given unlimited resources, would you recommend a policy in your country based on the criteria for screening?

When looking for relevant publications you may like to use the following key words: colorectal carcinoma; adenomatous polyps; faecal occult blood test (FOBT); flexible sigmoidoscopy; colonoscopy.

↻ **Feedback**

The first step is to review the accepted criteria for screening. Use the WHO criteria in the chapter to look at the disease, the test and the available treatment options.

You should first consider the burden of the disease in your own country. Although country-specific prevalence and incidence data may not be available, you could use data on hospital admissions, for example, to make inferences about your population. Colorectal cancer is the second most common cause of cancer deaths in the UK. An annual increase in incidence of colorectal cancer has been observed in a number of industrialized nations.

The next question is how much we know about the natural history of the condition. In the case of colorectal cancer, there is good evidence that the disease pathway begins with the development of benign colonic polyps, a proportion of which will develop into cancers under certain genetic and environmental conditions. Therefore it is possible to prevent the development of colorectal cancer by detecting and removing polyps in the benign latent phase of the disease, which is thought to last about 10 years.

We have described a pre-disease state, but are there any tests available to detect it? Looking at the literature, you will have learned about the detection of faecal occult blood (FOB). A simple FOB test, which patients find acceptable, has been shown in a number of randomized trials to reduce mortality from colorectal cancer in the general population. FOB testing has its limitations, however, as it has been found in trials to detect only a small proportion of screen-detected cancers. Refinements to the test currently used may improve the sensitivity of the test, but are there any other more sensitive methods?

You will also have read about endoscopic techniques (flexible sigmoidoscopy and colonoscopy), which can be used to look for bowel polyps and remove them before they become malignant. Endoscopy can also detect and biopsy cancerous lesions. This screening will probably detect more than 90–95% of cancers and large polyps at an earlier stage and thus reduce mortality from colorectal cancer. What are the pros and cons of these more sensitive tests? A limitation of screening with sigmoidoscopy is that a proportion of cancers will develop in the segment of bowel that cannot be reached by the sigmoidoscope. A colonoscope can be used to examine the entire rectum and colon but incurs an increased risk of bowel perforation, which is a very serious compli-cation. As we have discussed in the chapter, screening will be ineffective if compliance is low; an invasive endoscopic test may reduce compliance to a screening programme as patients are likely to find this test uncomfortable.

Once cancers and pre-cancers are detected, can we treat them? Evidence suggests that surgical removal of polyps and early cancers will have a significant impact on the morbidity and mortality associated with the disease compared with the treatment of established colorectal cancer, which still has a 5-year survival of just 40%.

A policy maker will also have to consider the resources needed to implement a screen-ing programme. In the case of endoscopic screening a large number of highly trained doctors and nurses will be needed to carry out screening, treatment, after-care and rehabilitation.

Summary

You should now be familiar with the statistical methods for evaluating the validity and reliability of screening and diagnostic tests. You should be able to describe and calculate the measures of validity of a test. You should also be able to explain the relationship between prevalence and predictive values. Finally, you should also know the WHO guidelines for initiating a screening programme and be able to review epidemiological data to make a decision as to the efficacy of screening for a particular disease.

References

Cochrane AL, Holland WW (1971) Validation of screening procedures. *British Medical Bulletin* 27(1): 3–8.

Cuckle HS, Wald NJ (1984) Principles of screening, in Wald NJ (ed) *Antenatal and Neonatal Screening*. Oxford: Oxford University Press.

Hakama M, Louhivuori K (1988) A screening programme for cervical cancer that worked. *Cancer Surveys* 7: 403–16.

Quinn M, Babb P, Jones J, Allen E (1999) Effect of screening on incidence of and mortality from cancer of cervix in England: evaluation based on routinely collected statistics. *British Medical Journal* 318: 904.

Sigurdsson K (1993) Effect of organized screening on the risk of cervical cancer. Evaluation of screening activity in Iceland, 1964–1991. *International Journal of Cancer* 54: 563–70.

Wilson JMG, Jungner G (1968) *Principles and Practice of Screening*. Geneva: World Health Organization.

Glossary

Absolute (attributable) risk A measure of association indicating on an absolute scale how much greater the frequency of diseases is in an exposed group than in an unexposed group, assuming the association between the exposure and disease is causal.

Aetiology The science or philosophy of causation.

Allocation concealment Method whereby the randomization schedule to allocate a treatment to participants in a randomized controlled trial is concealed from the investigator assessing patients for inclusion to prevent selection bias occurring.

Analytical study Study designed to test a hypothesis – for example, to examine whether a certain exposure is a risk factor for a particular disease.

Association Statistical dependence between two or more events, characteristics, or other variables. The presence of an association does not necessarily imply a causal relationship.

Attributable (absolute) risk fraction The proportion of disease among the exposed group that is attributable to the exposure.

Bias Any error that results in a systematic deviation from the estimation of the association between exposure and outcome.

Blinding Blinding or masking is the method used in a study in which observers and/or subjects are kept ignorant of the group to which the subjects are assigned. Where both observer and subjects are kept ignorant, the study is termed a double-blind study. If the statistical analysis is also done in ignorance of the group to which subjects belong, the study is sometimes described as triple-blind.

Cases Individuals in a population who have the outcome of interest (e.g. disease, health disorder, or event such as heart attack or death). Case definition should include clearly defined inclusion and exclusion criteria.

Case–control study An observational study starting with the identification of a group of cases and controls. The level of exposure to the risk factor of interest can then be measured (retrospectively) and compared.

Causality The relating of causes to the effects they produce. Most of epidemiology concerns causality, and several types of causes can be distinguished.

Chance The possibility that the results of an epidemiological study are due to chance alone rather than the truth.

Clinical trial An intervention study in which the unit of allocation to the different groups is the individual. The allocation of patients to the intervention may be random or not.

Cluster randomized controlled trial An intervention study in which groups of individuals (clusters) rather than individuals are randomized to an intervention.

Cohort study A follow-up observational study where groups of individuals are defined on the basis of their exposure to a certain suspected risk factor for a disease.

Comparison group Any group to which the index group is compared. Usually synonymous with control group.

Confidence interval The range of numerical values in which the population value being estimated is likely to be found. Confidence intervals indicate the strength of evidence; where confidence intervals are wide, they indicate less precise estimates of effect.

Confounding Situation in which an estimate of the association between a risk factor (exposure) and outcome is distorted because of the association of the exposure with another risk factor (a confounding variable) for the outcome under study.

Confounding variable (Confounder) A variable that is associated with the exposure under study and is also a risk factor for the outcome in its own right.

Controls (in a case-control study) Individuals who do not have the outcome of interest, and used as a comparison group in analytical studies.

Cross-sectional study A study design where exposure and outcome are measured at the same time.

Crude rate The rate in the population unadjusted for age, sex or other characteristics.

Descriptive study Study designed to describe the distribution of variables in a population without regard to causal or other hypotheses.

Determinant Any factor that effects a change in a health condition or other characteristic.

Diagnostic accuracy The accuracy of a test refers to the level of agreement between the test result and the 'true' clinical state.

Ecological fallacy The effects measured in groups may not be applicable at the level of individuals.

Ecological study A study in which the units of analysis are populations of groups of people rather than individuals.

Effectiveness The extent to which an intervention produces a beneficial result under usual conditions.

Efficacy The extent to which an intervention produces a beneficial result under ideal conditions.

Epidemiology The study of the distribution and determinants of health states or events in specified populations, and the application of this study to the control of health problems.

Exclusion criteria Conditions which preclude entrance of people into a study even if they meet the inclusion criteria for being a case.

Exposed Individuals in a study who have been exposed to or possess a characteristic that is a risk factor for a particular disease.

External validity (generalisability) The extent to which the results of a study can be generalized to the population from which the sample was drawn.

Follow-up Observation over a period of time of an individual, group, or initially defined population whose relevant characteristics have been assessed in order to observe changes in health status or health-related variables.

Gold standard A method, procedure, or measurement that is widely accepted as being the best available (nearest the truth).

Healthy worker effect Workers tend to have lower morbidity and mortality rates than the general population because people in employment are by definition healthier than the population as a whole, which includes people who are too ill to work.

Hypothesis A supposition which is phrased in such a way as to allow it to be tested and confirmed or refuted.

Incidence The frequency of new cases in a defined population during a specified period of time.

Incidence risk Calculated by dividing the number of new cases of a disease in a specified time period by the total person-time at risk during that period.

Incubation period The delay between exposure to the cause of a disease and the diagnosis (or first detectable symptom) of a disease.

Internal validity The extent to which the results of a study are not affected by bias and confounding.

Intervention study A study designed to test a hypothesis that there is a causal relationship between two variables, by modifying the putative causal factor in the population and observing the effect on the outcome.

Interviewer bias Systematic error due to an interviewer's subconscious or conscious gathering of selective data.

Latency period The time interval between disease occurrence and detection.

Matching A technique used to adjust for the effects of confounding. Controls are selected in such a way that the distribution of potential confounders among the controls is similar to the cases.

Measurement bias Systematic error in measurement or classification of the participants in a study.

Misclassification Incorrect determination of an individual's disease status, exposure status or both.

Negative predictive value The proportion of people who truly do not have the disease or risk factor among those who have a negative result in a screening/diagnostic test.

Non-response bias Systematic error due to the differences in response rate of participants in a study; a form of selection bias.

Null hypothesis A hypothesis of no association between exposure (or intervention) and outcome (disease state).

Observational study Epidemiological study in which the role of the investigator is observers what happens in the real world.

Observer bias A type of measurement bias that occurs when data gathering is influenced by knowledge of the exposure (or disease) status of the patient.

Odds (of disease) The ratio of the probability of getting the disease to the probability of not getting the disease during a given time period.

Odds (of exposure) The ratio of the probability of having been exposed to a particular risk factor to the probability of not having been exposed.

Odds ratio In a cohort study, the odds of disease in the exposed divided by the odds of disease in the unexposed. In a case–control study, the odds of exposure in the cases divided by the odds of exposure in the controls.

P- value The probability that an outcome as large as or larger than that observed would occur in a properly designed, executed, and analysed analytical study if in reality the null hypothesis were true.

Person-time at risk A measurement combining the number of people and time observed, used as a denominator in the calculation of rates. Represents the sum of each individual's time at risk.

Placebo An inert medicine or procedure that can be given to the control group in an intervention study.

Population attributable fraction (population attributable risk per cent) The proportion of disease in the study population that is attributable to the exposure.

Population attributable risk An estimate of the excess risk of disease in the total study population (of exposed and unexposed individuals) attributable to the exposure.

Positive predictive value The proportion of people who truly do have a disease or risk factor among those who have a positive result in a screening/diagnostic test.

Precision The accuracy or precision of an estimate of a value.

Prevalence The frequency of existing cases in a defined population at a particular point in time (point prevalence), or over a given period of time (period prevalence), as a proportion of the total population.

Primary prevention Measures taken to prevent the onset of illnesses and injury.

Prognosis The possible outcomes of a disease or condition and the likelihood that each one will occur.

Prognostic factor Factors associated with a condition's outcomes that predict the eventual development of those outcomes.

Prospective study Study in which data are collected in an ongoing way during the study.

Random error The variation of an observed value from the true population value due to chance alone.

Random sample A group of subjects selected from a population in a random manner (i.e. each member of the population has an equal chance of being selected).

Randomization The process of allocating patients to treatment based on chance. It is not possible for the investigator, clinician or patient to predict the allocation in advance.

Randomized controlled trial Study design where interventions, are assigned by random allocation rather than by conscious decisions of clinicians or patients.

Rate A ratio in which the denominator is expressed in units of person-time at risk.

Rate difference The absolute difference in the incidence rate between a group of individuals exposed and a group not exposed.

Rate ratio The ratio of the incidence rate in an exposed group to the incidence rate in an unexposed group.

Recall bias Systematic error due to the differences in accuracy or completeness of recall or memory of past events or experiences; a type of measurement bias.

Relative risk Relative measure of risk estimating the magnitude of association between an exposure and disease (or other outcome) indicating the likelihood of developing the disease in those exposed relative to those unexposed.

Repeatability A test or measure is repeatable if the results are identical or closely similar each time it is conducted under the same conditions.

Representative sample A sample that has the same characteristics as the population from which it was drawn and which it represents.

Responder bias A type of measurement bias that occurs when the information given by a participant is not independent of their exposure (or disease) status.

Response rate The proportion of those sampled who responded and returned a questionnaire or who participated in an interview divided by the total people who were eligible to complete/participate.

Retrospective data collection Data on disease status or exposure status are collected after the events have occurred (as opposed to prospective data collection).

Risk The proportion of people in a population initially free of disease who develop the disease within a specified time interval (the probability that an event will occur within a specified time).

Risk factor Patient characteristic (either inherited, such as a blood group, or behavioural, such as smoking and diet habits) or environmental factors (such as exposure to asbestos) associated with an increased or decreased probability (risk) of developing a disease (or other outcome).

Risk ratio An environmental exposure or inherited characteristic which is thought to be associated with an increased or decreased probability of occurrence of disease or other specified health outcome.

Sample size The number of individuals in a group under study.

Screening The organized attempt to detect, among apparently healthy people in the community, disorders or risk factors of which they are unaware.

Secondary prevention Measures to detect presymptomatic disease where early detection will mean a better outcome.

Selection bias Systematic differences in characteristics of the participants in a study between the study and control groups, so that they differ from each other by one or more factors that may affect the outcome of the study.

Sensitivity The proportion of 'true positives' correctly identified by a test. If the sensitivity is low, it suggests that a substantial number of positives have been missed. These are the 'false negatives'.

Specificity The proportion of 'true negatives' correctly identified by a test. The specificity is low if the proportion of 'false positives' is high.

Standardized mortality ratio (SMR) An indicator of the frequency of deaths in a population that takes into account the age and sex structure of the population.

Statistical power The statistical probability of detecting the minimum difference if a difference of that magnitude or greater truly exists.

Stratification The process or result of separating a sample into several subsamples according to specified criteria such as age groups or socioeconomic status.

Tertiary prevention Measures to reduce the disability from existing illnesses and prevent it from getting worse.

True prevalence Proportion of people in the population who really do have the disease in question, regardless of their test result. From a test result point of view, it includes the 'true' positives and the 'false' negatives.

Index

Abdulla, S., 54–7
absolute risk, 40–3, 47, 152
active surveillance, 124
acute rheumatic fever (ARF), 130
aetiological strength, 36
aetiology, 152
age
  maternal and Down's
    syndrome, 115–16, 120, 121
  smoking and mortality in British
    doctors, 70, 72
age-specific rates, 26–7, 29–31,
  130
agent, 7
alcohol
  and breast cancer, 61–3, 80–5
  and heart disease, 109, 121
allocation concealment, 89, 93,
  152
allocation of treatment regimens,
  88–90, 95
amniocentesis test, 141
anaemia, 55–6, 56–7
analogy, 110
analysis
  case-control studies, 78–9
  cohort studies, 68–9
  cross-sectional studies, 53–4
  ecological studies, 60–1
  intervention studies, 91
  see also interpretation
analytical studies, 152
  cohort studies, 68
  cross-sectional studies, 50, 51–2
  ecological, 59
Argentina, 26, 27, 27–8
assessment bias, 146
association, 34–49, 103, 152
  absolute measures, 40–3
  interpretation see interpretation
  measures of exposure effect and
    impact, 35–43
  relative measures, 35–9
  selection of appropriate measure
    for study design, 43–9
  strength of, 109

attributable (absolute) risk
  fraction, 40–1, 152
attributable risk see absolute risk
attributable risk per cent, 40, 48
Australia, 130

baseline data, 68, 124–5
Betrán, A.P., 131
bias, 98, 98–102, 107–8, 152
  case-control studies, 75, 76, 78,
    79, 98, 102
  cohort studies, 66–7, 68, 71, 99
  cross-sectional studies, 51–2
  ecological fallacy, 61, 132, 154
  ecological studies, 61
  enhancing value of routine data,
    133
  intervention studies, 88, 93, 95,
    98
  see also under individual types of
    bias
binary variables, 53
biological plausibility, 109
birth cohorts, 132
blinding (masking), 88, 89, 102,
  152
blocked randomization, 89
body mass index, 119
bowel polyps, 114, 150
Bradford Hill, A., 108
breast cancer, 145
  alcohol and, 61–3, 80–5
breast-feeding, 131
burden of disease, relative, 143

cancer
  age-specific rates, 26–7
  mortality rates, 27–8
  screening, 145
  see also under individual types of
    cancer
cancer registers, 129
cardiac mortality, 125
case-ascertainment bias, 125
case-control studies, 37, 44, 45,
  74–85, 152

alcohol consumption and breast
  cancer, 80–5
  analysis, 78–9
  hypothesis, 75
  information bias, 102
  interpretation, 79
  matching, 77, 79, 106
  measuring exposures, 78
  potential biases when
    evaluating screening, 146
  selection bias, 75, 76, 79, 98
  selection of cases, 75–6, 81
  selection of controls, 76–7
  strengths and weaknesses, 79–80
  study design, 74–7
case definition, 4–5, 19–20, 52–3,
  75, 152
cases, 5, 20, 152
categorical variables, 53
causality, 6, 97–8, 152
  criteria, 69, 108–10
  determining cause-effect
    relationship, 108–12
causation, models of, 7–9
cause of death, 127
censuses, 126
Centers for Disease Control and
  Prevention (USA), 128
central randomization, 89
Centre for Disease Surveillance
  and Control (CDSC) (UK), 128
cervical cancer, 146
chance (random error), 68, 85, 98,
  106–8, 152, 157
child mortality, 128
chlamydia, 131
cholera, 128
  John Snow's studies, 11–18, 109,
    123
Clark, E.G., 114
clinical criteria, 4
clinical disease stage, 9
clinical significance, 92
clinical trials (therapeutic studies),
  87, 152
  see also intervention studies